# Say Good-bye to Discouragement!

### How to Beat the Blues with the Word of God and the Power of the Holy Spirit

# Say Good-bye to Discouragement!

## How to Beat the Blues with the Word of God and the Power of the Holy Spirit

*by*
*Nancy Gray*

**Harrison House**
Tulsa, Oklahoma

Unless otherwise indicated, all Scripture quotations are taken from the *King James Version* of the Bible.

Scripture quotations marked AMP are taken from *The Amplified Bible. Old Testament* copyright © 1965, 1987 by Zondervan Corporation, Grand Rapids, MI. *New Testament* copyright © 1958, 1987 by The Lockman Foundation, La Habra, California. Used by permission.

Scripture quotations marked NAS are taken from the *New American Standard Bible.* Copyright © The Lockman Foundation 1960, 1962, 1963, 1968, 1971, 1972, 1973, 1975, 1977. Used by permission.

2nd Printing

*Say Good-bye to Discouragement!*
*How to Beat the Blues with the Word of God*
*and the Power of the Holy Spirit*
ISBN 0-89274-993-8
Copyright © 1996 by Nancy Gray
P. O. Box 470171
Tulsa, Oklahoma 74147

Published by Harrison House, Inc.
P. O. Box 35035
Tulsa, Oklahoma 74153

Printed in the United States of America.
All rights reserved under International Copyright Law. Contents and/or cover may not be reproduced in whole or in part in any form without the express written consent of the Publisher.

# Dedication

I wish to dedicate this book to a generous, kind and loving man, who stood with me as I grew up and now stands with me as I give out to others. He does everything in this ministry except the preaching, which enables me to fulfill the call on my life. He is my love and my friend, my husband Don.

# Contents

Preface

1 The Definition of Discouragement   15

2 Elijah: Discouragement From the Sayings of Others   29

3 Moses: Discouragement From the Burden of Responsibility   51

4 Reuben and Gad: Discouragement From Settling for the Suitable   73

5 Israel: Discouragement From Troubles Along the Way   97

6 David: Discouragement From Rebellion   119

Conclusion: Comfort and Counsel of the Holy Spirit

# Preface

**Now hope does not disapoint, because the love of God has been poured out in our hearts by the Holy Spirit who was given to us.**

**Romans 5:5**

Room 204 was quiet as I looked out at the warm April day. It was beautiful to see the new life springing up everywhere as a reminder of the season of life that always follows death.

The Stephens family had certainly had their share of death in the last year. We had lost a sister, Lois, in April of 1994 and another sister, Sally, in August of the same year. Now in April 1995 we were sitting in the hospital with our mother. We had been told that things were not going well for her, and we knew that the time was near for her to join the rest of our family at home in heaven.

A short time earlier, our family had consisted of eight members, seven children (six girls and one boy) and our mother. Our father had passed away in 1967. In one year's time, we were reduced to a family of five. Losing three members in such a short period would certainly be a huge blow to any family, but to one as close as ours the loss was devastating. It caused much discouragement, despair and depression.

Lois and I had been very close, both as sisters and as friends. I was also her *spiritual parent* in the Lord. At the time of her death, I experienced feelings I had never had to deal with before. It was quite a shock to lose a peer with whom I had shared, through the years, so much of my life and thoughts.

My sister and I had confided a great deal in each other. In that period of grief, I experienced shock, anger, disbelief and loneliness, to name only a few emotions. Not only did I have to deal with all that, but I also had to deal with guilt and uncertainty.

The devil was there to attack me in my time of distress. Questions continually plagued my mind. "Did I pray enough? Did I do all I could? Could I have done more for her?"

Since I felt that Lois had always looked to me for support, it was a time of inner frustration, remorse, regret and turmoil. The devil added his torment by bombarding my mind day and night.

One night, at about two or three in the morning, I awoke to the attack of such raging thoughts as, "Could I have done more, prayed more, cared more?" I got up to leave the bedroom, but as I started around the foot of the bed, I was arrested by the Holy Spirit.

In the Bible, the Holy Spirit is called the Comforter and the Counselor. He is willing and able to be with us and help us in any situation if we will call on Him.

I had been praying and calling on the Lord through all of those dark hours. In fact, I was praying as I rounded the end of the bed and was interrupted in thought by the Holy Spirit. He ministered to me until I was assured that I had done all I could for Lois. He let me know that I could not have done any more than I had done, and that ultimately it is the responsibility of each individual to establish and maintain his or her own walk with God. It is impossible for me, or anyone else, to *carry* another person through life in a personal relationship with the Lord.

Without thinking it through, I had not realized that I had been taking responsibility for another person's death.

We must not do that! We must do all we know to do, then we must stand believing. When all is said and done, responsibility rests with the individual and God. It would be a very burdensome journey through life if we had to be responsible for what happens in everyone else's lives.

Clearly, you and I are not the Messiah. We cannot save, heal or pay the price for anyone. We can only do what God has given us the weapons and resources to do. We must all develop our own relationship with the Lord, follow our own walk with Him and exercise our own faith in Him. We must stand one with another, but we must always depend on and look to God for the answers we need in our daily lives.

At the time of her passing, I did not know what transpired between Lois and God. I did not know what her innermost thoughts were, and I won't know until I meet with her in heaven. The realization of that fact was the beginning of healing within me.

In the same way, the Holy Spirit will begin healing and will initiate the release of confusion in your life, if you will call on and follow Him.

As the Holy Spirit was walking me toward complete healing, my sister Sally (the "baby" in our family and the sister just younger than I) was diagnosed with cancer. In just three short months after the death of Lois, Sally was gone too.

We were all in shock; it was as if someone had rubbed salt in an open wound. Everyone loved Sally because of her fun-loving nature. She laughed often and was a very caring, giving person.

Each family member has his or her own experiences and stories to tell about Sally, but as for me, there are many memories of her *growing up* years. I remember when she learned to drive and the time she and her fiancee came to tell me they were engaged, before telling anyone else. She stayed with me when I needed help with my new babies; there are so many good memories. What a shock for someone with such vitality and youth (she was just in her forties) to be suddenly taken away.

The emotions started all over again. We had not even healed from the first loss; now our hurt seemed doubled in intensity. It was as though we had been knocked down and in getting up had been knocked down again; only this time the effect was worsened by our weakened state. I did not experience the guilt this time, but the other emotions were the same and were made more raw by the second blow. I became extremely discouraged and was close to depression.

Again, I began to call upon the One within me, the Holy Spirit, of Whom Jesus spoke in John 15:26,16 AMP:

> But when the Comforter (Counselor, Helper, Advocate, Intercessor, Strengthener, Standby) comes, Whom I will send to you from the Father, the Spirit of Truth Who comes (proceeds) from the Father, He [Himself] will testify regarding Me.
>
> ...so that whatever you ask the Father in My Name [as presenting all that I AM], He may give it to you.

I cannot tell you that the emotional turmoil over losing yet another sister was gone instantly, or that I did not have to deal with loneliness and grief, but I can tell you that as I drew on the Holy Spirit, the healing was manifested more each week.

Then, just one year later, we found ourselves in Room 204 grieving over the impending death of our mother. We were all with her in those last weeks, not wanting to leave her alone and seeking to do all we could for her.

During that difficult time, someone said to me, "You children are so attentive to your mother. You sure take good care of her."

To this remark I replied, "She was attentive to us and took good care of us while we were young, so it is the least we can do."

What we did for our mother was nothing more than what she had done, in days gone by, for all of us.

In Room 204, as a family we ate together, slept together, laughed together and cried together; we shared our grief and our faith, drawing strength from one another and growing in love.

So it was that in April of 1995, my mother joined her loved ones in heaven. We now have family on both sides, in heaven and on earth. We shall enjoy those who reside on earth with us, but we look forward to our reunion in heaven. For just as they shout the victory in heaven, we can shout the victory on earth, and one day we shall *all* shout the victory together once again!

When you lose that many family members in such a short time it creates an emotional upheaval that is difficult to understand, much less to describe. Once more there was salt in the wound and a feeling of not quite being able to get up before being knocked down again. We never had the normal time to adjust to each death, so the weight of all the losses seemed to pile one upon the other. Thank God for the Holy Spirit!

In these pages, I have shared a portion of my life with you so that you will know that in time of discouragement, despondency and depression people can help in a *measure*. However, if you are born again, you have the *Comforter* — the Counselor, Helper, Advocate, Intercessor, Strengthener and Standby — within you. You must look to God and pray for His character and attributes to rise up and minister to you by the Holy Spirit. He is always available to you. He will always listen and be there for you.

No matter how nice and well-intentioned the people around you may be, *no one* understands like Jesus. *No one* comforts like the Holy Spirit. *No one* stands with you like God. He has said, "I will never leave you nor forsake you." (Heb. 13:5.) When discouragement comes, let me encourage you to look to God, Who dwells with you. Only He can bring you from the defeat of discouragement to the victory in Christ.

# 1
# The Definition of Discouragement

How does discouragement become depression and, ultimately, deep despair? Many people do not understand that discouragement is a subtle attack against them and, more importantly, against their Christianity. Without understanding the danger of discouragement, believers will fight ineffectively, using the wrong weapons.

Often Christians do not even stand against discouragement as they should, because they don't perceive it for what it really is — a threat to their Christian walk. Consequently, not recognizing the subtlety and danger of it, they allow discouragement to continue to develop in their lives until it evolves into despondency, and then depression.

Join with me as we uncover the *discouragement deception*. See how cunningly it can invade your life and how absolutely deadly it is. Once the magnitude of this harmful influence has been revealed and you discover how to stand against it, you can put it out of your life. Then as you allow the joy of the Lord to be your strength (Neh. 8:10), it will shine through your countenance.

## What Is Discouragement?

What is discouragement? The *New American Standard Bible* tells us that discouragement is the "depression of one's spirits."[1]

---

[1] *New American Standard Bible,* The New Open Bible Study Edition (Nashville: Thomas Nelson Publishers, 1990), "Topical Index," p. 115.

This definition suggests that when we are discouraged, it is as though we are being pushed down on the *inside*. Eventually, without our really knowing what is happening to us, depression then develops into a sense of hopelessness that drags us down into the pit of despondency and despair.

> **Hope deferred maketh the heart *sick*: but when the desire cometh, it is a tree of life.**
>
> **Proverbs 13:12**

The word sick here means to be wounded, weak or infirm.[2] So we find that the depression of our spirit, the discouragement that is pushing us down on the inside, can even have an outward physical effect upon us, if we do not take steps to resist the influence coming against us.

Webster's dictionary tells us that to *discourage* is to "deprive of courage."[3] So discouragement leaves us with an inability to deal with danger, trouble or pain. The walk that God has planned for each of us will, ultimately, be greatly inhibited by the presence of fear. Without courage, we will not be able to fulfill the call of God on our lives.

## Discouragement Neutralizes

In the King James Bible, *nuw'*, one of the Hebrew words translated *discouraged*, means to "forbid, dissuade, or neutralize."[4] Again, discouragement is designed to stop us, and it is not something to be taken lightly. Not only can it hinder our witnessing and prevent us from touching other people's lives, it can also limit us in our capacity for success in fulfilling the call of God. The devil's purpose in sending discouragement upon us is to *neutralize* us.

At one time, I was a cosmetologist, and in that profession I gave a lot of permanents. Anyone who has

---

[2]James Strong, *Strong's Exhaustive Concordance of the Bible* (Nashville: Abingdon, 1890), "Hebrew and Chaldee Dictionary," p. 39, entry #2470.

[3]*Webster's New World Dictionary, Concise Edition*, s.v. "discourage."

[4]Strong, p. 77, entry #5106.

## The Definition of Discouragement

given a permanent understands that to neutralize means to stop an action. When the hair is rolled on a permanent rod and the permanent solution is applied, a chemical process is set into motion. That process breaks down the hair linkage and causes it to conform to the rods on which it is rolled, whether large or small. When the hair reaches the desired state of curl, then on goes the neutralizer. As the neutralizer saturates each hair conformed on the rods, *the process is stopped.*

When the devil uses discouragement in your life, it is to neutralize you, to stop your activity.

At some time in the past, you may have come to a place where you surrendered your life to God. As He gently prepared your heart and brought you to a desired state in which to serve Him better, the enemy came along and poured on discouragement, the neutralizer.

That neutralizer, in the form of discouragement, is geared to stop you from being active. Once you are effectively neutralized, then your ability to reach people by preaching and witnessing, by speaking and teaching the Word of God, and by living in and for Him, will come to a screeching halt. When your forward progress is stopped, you will no longer advance, and you may even go backward.

## Discouragement Curtails

Not only is discouragement sent by Satan to impede our forward movement, but also to completely immobilize us.

*Qatsar,* another of the Hebrew words translated *discouraged* in the Bible, means to "cut down," "curtail" or "dock off."[5] Have you ever seen the breed of small dogs that have almost no tails at all because they have been "docked off" or cut short for generations?

---

[5]Strong, p. 104, entry #7114.

With this visual definition in mind, discouragement could be interpreted to include cutting short your ministry, cutting short your life, cutting short your witness — thus minimizing the work that God has for you to do.

Discouragement is a tool used by the devil to cut you down to size and to totally overcome you so that you take your eyes off God and focus on your problem. If allowed to do so, discouragement will come between you and the plan God has for you.

Even though discouragement is very subtle, it is quite deadly. When it comes, there is always a mourning process, a grieving over things that seem to have been lost.

Because the purpose of discouragement is to trouble you, when you become discouraged you don't seem to be able to go forward. You may even begin to look back to past accomplishments and the positive influence you once had on people. As you do so, the weight of grieving over that loss may neutralize you and cause you to stop and stand still. Standing still will put a halt to your activity. It will hinder your forward progress toward your own wellness and your ministry to others in need.

Discouragement is such a negative force that you may start to speak negative things. Once you begin to dwell on the negative, trouble will come down on you and cause harmful effects in your life. Hope deferred will distress you by making your heart sick, causing you to feel wounded, weak or infirm.

Although it is not a sin to experience moments of temporary discouragement, I believe we become accountable for it when we *yield* to it, allowing it to *keep us out of the will of God*.

## Discouragement Breaks Down

*Chathath,* still another Hebrew word translated *discouraged* in the *King James Version*, means "to break down, either (lit.) by violence, or (fig.) by confusion or fear: — (be (make) afraid,...(cause to) dismay,...scare, terrify."[6]

Discouragement will "break down" the door to your mind and heart and allow violence, confusion and fear to come in. When violence comes against you, fear and confusion will begin to overtake you. Many times it will have such an adverse effect on your nervous system that you will fall apart.

Discouragement left unchecked evolves into despondency, then into depression and eventually into mental stress and even emotional collapse.

The devil does not want you to be whole. Wholeness is from God. Satan will subtlety come in and deceptively try to steal from you all that God has given you to make you whole, as well as holy. The objective is to *beat you down*.

When the devil comes with discouragement, he will use it as a whip. It will be as if no matter what you do, no matter where you go, you are being whipped with discouragement and, in fact, in that sense you *are* the *whipping boy* of discouragement.

The devil uses discouragement in a most subtle and deceptive way. However, it is so potentially dangerous that you need to resist it with everything that is within you and in heaven — meaning Jesus Christ, the Holy Spirit and the Word of God. Not only does discouragement cause you to become ineffective for God, the effects of discouragement can frighten or terrify you, which will also in turn lead to despondency, depression and emotional collapse.

## Discouragement "Liquefies"

Again based on one of the Hebrew words *macac* translated *discouraged* in the Old Testament, we have

---

[6]Strong, p. 45, entry #2865.

discouragement defined as, "to liquefy; fig. to waste (with disease), to faint (with fatigue, fear or grief),...melt (away)."[7]

The results of discouragement can "liquefy" you.

For instance, pour water on a counter top. What happens? That water conforms to the flat surface on which it is poured. Take that same water and put it in a cup. The liquid conforms to the cylindrical shape of the cup. You can put water on any surface or pour it into any container and it will take the form onto or into which it is placed.

If you take an ice cube out of the refrigerator or the freezer and place it on a flat surface, it will melt and conform to the flat surface. If the ice cube melts in a glass cup, it will conform to the cylinder shape. That is what the pressure of discouragement can do to you; it can cause you to conform to the world around you by "melting" you down and causing you to conform to your surroundings.

The Scriptures tell us not to conform to our earthly surroundings:

> **And be not conformed to this world: but be ye transformed by the renewing of your mind, that ye may prove what is that good, and acceptable, and perfect, will of God.**
>
> **Romans 12:2**

Do not be conformed; do not allow discouragement to liquefy you, to "melt" you down, to pour you out emotionally so that you conform to your surroundings.

In Romans 12:2, when the Apostle Paul says not to be conformed to this world, but to be transformed by the renewing of your mind, the Greek word translated *conformed* in the English Bible means "to fashion alike, i.e. to conform to the same pattern."[8]

---

[7]Strong, p. 69, entry #4549.

[8]Strong, "Greek Dictionary of the New Testament," p. 70, entry #4964.

## The Definition of Discouragement

To me, being molded or fashioned to fit a conformed pattern requires pressure applied by some outside influence. Thus this verse says to me that we are not to be pressured into fitting into this world's system or age.

We should strive not to conform to this world, but to transform ourselves by the renewing of our minds. By renewing our minds to the Word of God, we cannot be pressured into fitting in with the world system.

If you take an ice cube and put it under the pressure of heat, it will lose its form and begin to conform to its surroundings. In the same way, when discouragement causes you to lose your form, you begin to waste away, to "liquefy."

I have seen discouraged people become so *liquefied* that they could not eat or sleep; they could not function because they had no form or strength.

As we have seen, to be *discouraged* also means "to faint (with fatigue)"[9] or weariness. Hope deferred makes the heart sick, wounded, weak or infirm. Being overcome with weariness will cause you to feel hopeless and to become weary in well doing. (2 Thess. 3:13.) Instead of standing firm and strong, you will begin to waste away and lose form by melting under discouragement.

Make a decision to believe God Who gives strength to the weary and increases the power of those who lack might. You will gain new strength and be able to run and not get tired, to walk and not become weary. (Is. 40:29,31 NAS.)

To conform is to lose form. To believe God is to be formed into the image of Christ through His Word.

## Discouragement Crushes and Oppresses

Another one of the biblical Hebrew words translated *discouraged* is *ratsats*, meaning "to crack in pieces, lit. or fig.:

---

[9]Strong, "Hebrew and Chaldee Dictionary," p. 69, entry #4549.

— break, bruise, crush,...oppress, struggle together."[10] As mentioned earlier, discouragement is geared to cause you to crumble and break down so that you will not be whole.

Here it is again.

The purpose of discouragement is to crack you in pieces so that you will no longer be whole. If you are not whole, then you will not be able to function the way God wants you to function.

When I saw discouragement defined as breaking, bruising, crushing, oppressing or struggling together, I could imagine an inward struggle in all of us. The pulling causes us to continually look back at what we have done, so that we are so discouraged we cannot go forward. Yet, there is a pulling of God to come forward, to come up higher. This conflict causes an inner struggle.

What does Paul tell the Philippians that he did about past struggles that would threaten to pull him down?

> **Brethren, I count not myself to have apprehended: but this one thing I do, forgetting those things which are behind, and reaching forth unto those things which are before,**
>
> **I press toward the mark for the prize of the high calling of God in Christ Jesus.**
>
> **Philippians 3:13,14**

As suggested by Paul in Philippians 3:15-17, we are to walk in the Truth we know and know the Truth we are to walk in. That is what you and I should do to offset the crushing burden of discouragement and to keep our spirits lifted.

Let us remember that the definition of discouragement also includes bruise, crush or oppress. We have those

---

[10]Strong, p. 110, entry #7533.

## The Definition of Discouragement

among us who do not "feel" or "see" themselves as whole as a result of being bruised, crushed or oppressed by the enemy, by other people or by the circumstances that surround them. Allow me to encourage you by stating that no matter what the enemy (Satan) or other people may say or do, or what the circumstances may be in which you find yourself, it has no bearing on the truth of God's Word.

If you are a child of God, Jesus bore your griefs (sicknesses), and carried your sorrows (pains). He was wounded for your transgressions, He was bruised for your iniquities; the chastisement of your peace was upon Him; and with His stripes you are healed. (Is. 53:4,5.) Jesus has already paid the price, so you can stop paying. You are free from the bruising, crushing and oppression that accompany discouragement.

Make a decision, "I will not accept this discouragement, but I will be encouraged in the healing that Jesus paid for, which makes me whole."

Discouragement steals the knowledge of the wholeness that Jesus paid for on the cross. If you allow it to do so, it will stop you by causing you to keep your mind on yourself and on the activity around you. Fight it by focusing your mind on the activity that took place on the cross and press on through the discouragement to victory in Him.

Remember, you are made whole through Jesus Christ.

## Discouragement Disheartens

To be discouraged is the same as being *disheartened*, which means "to...lose hope,"[11] or confidence, which leads to negativism and disapproval. You will find that discouraged people quickly become very negative people.

---

[11] *Webster's New World Dictionary, Young People's Edition*, s.v. "dishearten."

To be *discouraged* is also to be "dispirited."[12] To be dispirited or spiritless is to be robbed of the Word of God. We find an example of this in the parable of the sower:

**The sower soweth the word.**

**And these are they by the way side, where the word is sown; but when they have heard, Satan cometh immediately, and taketh away the word that was sown in their hearts.**

**Mark 4:14,15**

The sower sows the Word, and immediately Satan comes to take away the Word. Therefore, to be spiritless is to be disheartened, without heart.

To be spiritless is to have the Word stolen. To be spiritual is to be full of the Word.

Some people are so discouraged that they are not even aware they are discouraged. They blame their condition on other people, and they call it other things; they just put the wrong title on it.

Only when we can see and understand discouragement can we know what our enemy is and begin to fight it. It is imperative to understand that the way of discouragement is subtle and the results of discouragement are dangerous. That is why we must resist it.

How? By staying full of the Word and prayer. Don't allow the Word to be stolen from you! If you do, you will lose hope, give up and faint: "Also [Jesus] told them a parable to the effect that they ought always to pray and not to turn coward (faint, lose heart, and give up)" (Luke 18:1 AMP).

Decide now to stay full of prayer and God's Word that you may be spiritual and not spiritless.

---

[12]W. E. Vine, *Vine's Expository Dictionary of Old and New Testament Words* (Old Tappan, NJ: Fleming H. Revell Company, 1981), Volume 1: A-Dys, "DISCOURAGE (-D)," p. 316.

## Discouragement Speaks

One important thing you will find out when you study the subject is that discouragement speaks. Discouragement has a language.

When you listen to people who are discouraged, or when you listen to yourself when you become discouraged, you will begin to pinpoint certain spoken similarities.

As we have seen, discouragement is negative, and it dwells on the negative. The language of discouragement says, for example:

"I want to give up."

"I want to quit."

"I've had it; someone else can do it a lot better than I can."

"I don't want to go to church; I don't want to get up out of bed and go to work."

Discouragement says:

"There's no one else who's going through what I'm going through."

"I'm all alone, and no one cares."

"I'm so miserable I just want to die."

I always say, if there were a theme song for discouragement it would be that old spiritual, "Nobody Knows the Trouble I've Seen." That is what discouraged people dwell on — trouble. They dwell upon the negative — whatever is causing them trouble — rather than the positive — the Word of God.

They need to sing the rest of that song — "Nobody knows *but Jesus.*"

Jesus knows what is happening to people but Satan deceptively brings them out of the Word, causing them to dwell on their discouragement. He neutralizes them and, in so doing, forbids and prevents them from going on. He "docks off" their ministry. He steals from them the Word of God, cutting them down to his size so he can fight and defeat them. He does all that because he knows that when they are in God, they can overrule him by the Word of God.

## Encouragement Overcomes

**Ye are of God, little children, and have overcome them: because greater is he that is in you, than he that is in the world.**

**1 John 4:4**

If God is for us, who can be against us? (Rom. 8:31.) We can add many other Scriptures to show that, together with God, we have the power to overcome the enemy.

Jesus came to earth and overcame the evil one. (1 John 3:8; Col. 2:15.) Because of our faith in Him and His finished work on Calvary, we have been translated out of the kingdom of darkness — the authority of Satan — and have been translated into the Kingdom of God's dear Son, Jesus Christ. (Col. 1:13.) Because greater is He Who is in us than he who is in the world, we too can overcome the evil one.

## Submit, Resist, and the Devil Will Flee

**Submit yourselves therefore to God. Resist the devil, and he will flee from you.**

**James 4:7**

This Scripture does not say that the devil will flee from *God*, it says that he will flee from *you*. Submit to God. Remain in His Word and in prayer. Know what His promises are and understand your relationship with Him.

By submitting yourself to God, you are resisting the devil. When you resist Satan in submission to God, he *must* flee from you. That is the order: 1) submission, 2) resistance and 3) fleeing.

## The Definition of Discouragement

You submit, you resist, he flees.

You can't just submit and expect the devil to flee from you. You can't just resist and expect him to flee. You must submit yourself to God and, in that submission, resist the devil; then he will flee from you.

The devil will curtail you, cut you short and neutralize you if he can break you down by confusion and fear or if he can liquefy you to get you to conform to your surroundings, the world around you. If Satan can just get you to faint with fatigue as you melt into whatever setting you find yourself, then he will have a good chance to overcome you.

Stay aware of the language of discouragement so you can hear and be able to pinpoint the tools of the enemy.

Discouraged people lose heart. They lose their drive. That's the depression of the spirit. That's the pushing down on the inside that we discussed at the beginning of this chapter. Once they are pushed down on the inside, they begin to lose heart. Their loss of enthusiasm and energy begins to manifest itself on the outside until, finally, they are broken down completely.

As I have studied and taught on discouragement, I have discovered what God can do in the midst of trial. When I needed His help, the Holy Spirit brought back to me not only the comfort of the Lord, but also the knowledge and wisdom of God.

He will do the same for you.

If we will allow Him to do so, our God can and will help us every time discouragement comes against us.

*Don't Quit!*

Discouragement is an enemy that cannot be taken lightly.

You have the weapons to be an overcomer, so do not let discouragement defeat you. Why? Because God is on your side, and you are a winner! Stay in the game until you win.

*Don't quit!*

As long as you and God are working together, you can survive. Don't allow discouragement to bring you down, but allow God to lift you up.

Make the decision — "I will believe God."

# 2
# Elijah: Discouragement From the Sayings of Others

Let's look at some discouraged people in the Bible and use them as our examples, as Paul wrote of the Israelites in his letter to the church in Corinth:

> **Now all these things happened unto them for ensamples: and they are written for our admonition, upon whom the ends of the world are come.**
> **1 Corinthians 10:11**

We will be able to see the things the Israelites did that were correct and right in line with God. We need to take heed of these good examples and follow them. The incorrect decisions that they made, decisions not in line with the Word of God, should be an example for us *not* to follow.

In looking at these people, we will see how they handled their difficult situations. We will be able to see a pattern of how to come out of discouragement, avoid despondency and resist depression. I believe that as we read their stories and study the Scriptures that relate them, we are going to change just as these people did. By gaining knowledge and then acting on that knowledge, we will become free!

As our first example of a man of God who became discouraged and, I believe, went right on into depression, let's look at the prophet Elijah. We begin his story in the nineteenth chapter of 1 Kings, at the end of a three-and-a-half year drought brought on Israel by God because of iniquity in the land.

## Elijah and the False Prophets

**Now Ahab told Jezebel all that Elijah had done, and how he had killed all the prophets with the sword.**
**1 Kings 19:1 NAS**

This verse reveals what King Ahab reported to his wife, the evil queen Jezebel, after his confrontation with Elijah. He was not totally truthful in relaying the events of the day.

In 1 Kings 18, we read how Elijah challenged the Israelites concerning their falling away from God, rebuking them for their compromise. He said to them, "How long will you hesitate between two opinions? If the Lord is God, follow Him; but if Baal, follow him." (v. 21.) The people did not answer.

Elijah had come to confront the people of Israel as well as King Ahab, their leader. Ahab had set the stage by calling together all Israel and the prophets of Baal to Mount Carmel. Elijah had simply told them that they could call on the name of their god and he would call on the name of the Lord. Then, the god who answered by fire, He was God. All the people agreed that this was a good idea.

The prophets of Baal made an altar, prepared an ox and called on the name of their god. They called from morning until noon, trying everything they could to get Baal to answer them; but to no avail. Elijah began to mock them regarding the obvious absence of their god. They cried out even louder and began to cut themselves according to their custom, until the blood gushed out. Mid-day passed and they prophesied until evening, but Baal did not respond, and no one else was paying attention to them.

Elijah called the people of Israel to come near him as he set up an altar. He took twelve stones, which corresponded to the number of the tribes of the sons of Jacob, and he built the altar in the name of the Lord. He made a trench around the altar large enough to hold two measures of seed. He arranged the wood and cut the ox in pieces, laying it on the wood. Four barrels of water were ordered to be poured over the sacrifice and on the wood. Elijah commanded that the pouring process be repeated two more times until the water flowed all around the altar, filling the trench that had been dug around it.

Elijah then called on God, saying, "...Lord God of Abraham, Isaac, and of Israel, let it be known this day that thou art God in Israel, and that I am thy servant, and that I have done all these things at thy word" (1 Kings 18:36). As a servant to the Most High, Elijah was calling on God to make Himself known to all those who were gathered there.

Elijah went on to proclaim, "Hear me, O Lord, hear me, that this people may know that thou art the Lord God, and that thou hast turned their heart back again" (v. 37). This was not a contest to determine who was the greater between two gods, but rather who was *the only true* God.

Immediately, the fire of the Lord fell, consuming the offering, the wood, the stones and the dust. It even licked up all the water that was in the trench. When the people saw it, they fell on their faces saying, "...The Lord, he is the God; the Lord, he is the God" (v. 39).

Elijah then commanded, "...Take the prophets of Baal; let not one of them escape..." (v. 40). The people did as he said and took the prophets to the brook Kishon, where they were all slain.

Afterwards, Elijah ordered King Ahab, "...Get thee up, eat and drink; for there is a sound of abundance of rain" (v. 41). And so it was that a basically clear sky turned black and produced a great rain.

Thus, the long drought finally ended.

## Elijah, Ahab and Jezebel

Ahab couldn't wait to get home and tell Jezebel how Elijah had killed all the prophets with the sword. He put the blame on Elijah and did not mention God's part in it.

That was so typical of Ahab.

Sometimes there are people in our lives who mean us harm. I believe that God is able to reveal to us who they are if we will listen to His voice.

Elijah had knowledge of Ahab's true character as it is described in 1 Kings 21. There we read how Ahab wanted the vineyards of Naboth, who refused to sell his inheritance to Ahab.

Faced with Naboth's refusal, Ahab became very sullen and vexed. He went home and lay down on his bed, turning his face to the wall. Noticing that her husband was not eating, Jezebel came in and asked, "How is it that your spirit is so solemn and that you are eating no food?"

"It's because I want Naboth's vineyard and he won't sell it to me," Ahab whined.

"Get up and eat and refresh yourself," said Jezebel, "I'm going to give you the vineyard of Naboth the Jezrelite."

Jezebel wrote a letter in Ahab's hand, sealed it with the king's seal and sent it to the elders of the nobles who were living with Naboth in his city. In these letters Jezebel ordered the elders to proclaim a fast and to seat Naboth at the head of the people. She sent lying witnesses to accuse Naboth, claiming that he had blasphemed against God and the king. Afterwards Naboth was taken out and stoned to death.

Then Jezebel went to her husband and said, "Okay, Ahab, here's the vineyard you wanted."

Ahab was the most evil man of his time, and Jezebel was the meanest woman of her age. Ahab knew what reaction he would get from Jezebel when he returned to blame Elijah for everything that had happened on Mount Carmel.

Many people get discouraged because there are around them those who unjustly accuse them or who put blame on them for something they did not do. That is exactly what happened to Elijah. He had just returned from a wonderful experience, a glorious victory. Nevertheless, we see how even in the midst of triumph, discouragement came and led him away toward defeat — all because of the wrath of an evil woman who was enraged at the death of her false prophets.

## Discouragement Through Sayings

**Then Jezebel sent a messenger unto Elijah, saying, So let the gods do to me, and more also, if I make not thy life as the life of one of them by to morrow about this time.**

**1 Kings 19:2**

One of the greatest ways of discouragement is through *sayings*. At a time of extreme success in his ministry, Elijah received a threatening message meant to invoke fear in his heart from Jezebel.

One of the definitions of the word discourage is to break down by fear. Fear can cause a nervous breakdown. Fear can cause people to do things that they would not normally do.

There will be times in your own life and ministry when you will be like Elijah. You will come out of a victory gained by being obedient to God, and Satan will send a message of fear to you. It will be something that will touch you deeply and strike at the very core of your heart. It will seem as though you have to make a decision right then. You will either move toward the fear that arises within you or you will move toward the faith that comes through the Word of God.

Such situations demand a conscious decision. Once you understand that fear comes to discourage you and to lead you from discouragement to despondency into depression, then you will run to God and not be afraid.

> Peace I leave with you, my peace I give unto you: not as the world giveth, give I unto you. Let not your heart be troubled, neither let it be afraid.
>
> John 14:27

Jesus has said that He has given us a peace that the world cannot counterfeit. We must stay in relationship with God to receive the peace that will deter discouragement. In times of stress and doubt, we must run to God and His Word, not away from Him or His people.

## Fear Leads to Flight

> And when he saw that, he arose, and went for his life, and came to Beersheba, which belongeth to Judah, and left his servant there.
>
> 1 Kings 19:3

Jezebel sent a *messenger of fear* to Elijah, just as Satan will send fear to you and me. He will try to take us from victory to defeat.

Did Elijah react to Jezebel's threat? Yes, he ran for his life. His safety became uppermost in his mind.

Fear will cause us to move toward discouragement, seeking shelter. In the same way, Elijah ran for his life "...and came to Beersheba, which belongeth to Judah, and left his servant there."

The breaking down of Elijah's ministry started by a cutting short, a curtailing and a neutralizing. A liquefying process began to take place. When he left his servant there at Beersheba, he separated himself from the last person who was in agreement with him. His servant not only understood Elijah, he also believed the same things that his master believed. Discouragement will separate us from those whom God has sent to help us, to serve us and to encourage us.

## "It's No Use, I'm Just No Good!"

> But he himself went a day's journey into the wilderness, and came and sat down under a juniper

**tree: and he requested for himself that he might die; and said, It is enough; now, O Lord, take away my life; for I am not better than my fathers."**

**1 Kings 19:4**

Elijah reacted to the messenger of fear with fear. When fear or any message of Satan comes and you react to it, you will find yourself in a wilderness area.

Never react, always act.

When you take action, you determine the direction that you are going. You decide what you will do.

When Elijah reacted, he began to move away from God's people. He left those who could help him, and his servant who understood and believed in him, and went to a wilderness area. He then sat down under a juniper tree and prayed that he might die.

Of course, God is not in the business of taking lives, but we see again that discouragement has a language. It is negative itself, and it dwells on the negative. Listen as discouragement gives way to despondency.

After Elijah had prayed to die, saying, "That's it, Lord, I've had it!" he felt discouraged and stripped of courage. He had had enough and wanted his life to end. He concluded his remarks by claiming, "I'm no better than my ancestors."

Another characteristic of discouragement is that it causes people to dwell upon their past. Elijah had gotten into a "pity party." He was feeling sorry for himself and cried, "Just let me die, Lord, because I'm no better than my ancestors. They made mistakes, and now that's what I've done. I will never change!"

If discouragement can get you to dwell on past mistakes, you will never move into the future with God. If it can get you to dwell on the negative, you will never move into the positive.

By dwelling on the past, Elijah began to think about things that were detrimental to him.

Discouragement will grab hold of your mind and consume it by causing you to dwell on things that will drag you into depression.

Using Paul as an example, we can be encouraged to leave the past behind:

> **Brethren, I count not myself to have apprehended: but this one thing I do, forgetting those things which are behind, and reaching forth unto those things which are before,**
>
> **I press toward the mark for the prize of the high calling of God in Christ Jesus.**
>
> Philippians 3:13,14

Look at this pattern of behavior. Elijah received the messenger of fear, he listened, and he became afraid.

When you give your ear to the messenger of fear, or anything opposite of what God says in His Word, then it will create within you an element of fear.

When Elijah became afraid, he reacted by going in the wrong direction. He then cut himself off from the people who could help him. When he cut himself off, he found himself in a wilderness area — a place without water and food. It was a dry place of discouragement, just a passageway to depression.

Once Elijah found himself in the wilderness, then he wanted to die. His feelings overcame him, and he requested that God kill him. He began to dwell on his past, on his fathers' mistakes and on his dismal situation in general. He did not realize that the reason he was there was because he had run away in fear, farther into discouragement.

When fear attacks, it plays with your mind. If you give into it by running from God, you will be running toward discouragement and despair. You will eventually run farther and farther and get deeper and deeper into trouble. These negative thoughts will take over your mind. That's why you should do as Paul did: *forget* the past and *press on* toward what lies ahead, which is the mark of the prize of God's calling for you.

Press on by getting into the Word of God and prayer.

## "Get Up and Eat!"

**And as he lay and slept under a juniper tree, behold, then an angel touched him, and said unto him, Arise and eat.**

**1 Kings 19:5**

Like many people in the depths of depression, Elijah just wanted to cover his head and go to sleep. So after dwelling on the past and asking God to take his life, he went to sleep under a juniper tree.

Many people can't sleep when they are depressed, but some people escape by sleeping. I believe that Elijah became so weary and tired from his emotional struggle that he had to lie down.

Whether it is through sleep, food, activity, wrong company, addictions or bad habits, discouragement will cause you to want to escape in some manner.

As Elijah slept under the juniper tree, an angel touched him and said to him, "Get up and eat." Of course, God had sent the angel, because He is in the business of helping us up and never pushing us down.

When you cry out to God and keep the lines of communication open to Him, He can come on the scene and begin to move on your behalf. Sometimes you don't see it, hear it or understand it, and it may not be in the form of an angel; but when you call out to God, He will answer you.

God sent an angel to touch Elijah. A touch from God in any form will encourage you to get up! All of us need a gentle touch from God, especially in the midst of discouraging situations.

An angel of God, a man of God or a woman of God are ones who will try to get you to come up higher. When anyone brings out the best in you so that you are motivated to come out of dejection, rejection, despondency, depression and discouragement — that is God in action!

In the touch from the angel there was a dictate from God to arise and eat. In essence He was saying to Elijah, "I will not kill you; I want you to get up, eat — and live."

When you get up and eat, it helps your body to stay alive. In the spiritual realm, when you eat of the Word of God, it causes you to stay alive spiritually. If you are discouraged today, you need to eat the Word of God. Arise, come up higher, and fill yourself, not only to stay alive spiritually, but to overcome natural problems.

## The Bread and the Water

**And he looked, and behold, there was a cake baken on the coals, and a cruse of water at his head. And he did eat and drink, and laid him down again.**

**1 Kings 19:6**

I think it is interesting that a bread cake was put right at Elijah's head.

God has given each of us a mind and He tells us to gird up our mind and use it. (1 Pet. 1:13.) We need the knowledge of the Word of God.

In John 6:35 Jesus says that *He* is the "bread of life." We are to partake of that bread daily.

Elijah's bread is a type or symbol of Christ, and it was baked on hot stones. The stones, in turn, are a type or symbol of the Word of God, as the good foundation rock Jesus spoke of in Matthew 7:24. We know from John 7:38 and 39 that water is a type or symbol of the Holy Spirit.

When the angel touched Elijah and told him to arise and eat, he told him what to eat. He placed at his head the type of Jesus Christ and the symbol of the Holy Spirit.

We need to have understanding and knowledge in our natural mind of Who Jesus is.

> **Is not my word like as a fire? saith the Lord; and like a hammer that breaketh the rock in pieces?**
> **Jeremiah 23:29**

When the knowledge of Jesus Christ is baked on the Word that is hot like fire, it is like a hammer that smashes all the evil in our hearts. If we are going to come out of discouragement, we need to center on Jesus. We need to allow our minds to dwell upon Him through the Word of God. We need to eat it and drink it, and allow the Holy Spirit to water it, so that the revelation of the knowledge goes from our heads to our hearts.

After Elijah ate, what did he do? He lay down again.

If you are not brought out of your discouraging situation immediately, don't get into more discouragement. God works according to His own plan and timetable. Don't dwell on your current circumstances, just eat a little more of the Word of God.

## "The Journey Is Too Great for Thee"

> **And the angel of the Lord came again the second time, and touched him, and said, Arise and eat: because the journey is too great for thee.**
> **1 Kings 19:7**

When Elijah lay down again, an angel of the Lord came a second time to awaken him and prepare him for what lay ahead.

God will touch us a second time, a third time and a fourth time. He will touch us until He gets us on our feet.

This time the angel of the Lord said, "Get up and eat, because the journey is too hard for you." The angel of the Lord was saying to Elijah that the journey before him was long and difficult and that Elijah could not make it alone, he had to depend upon the strength of the Lord.

Like Elijah, if we are to face the hardships of our life's journey, we must have the knowledge of God, baked by the Word and watered by the Holy Spirit. So many people are praying for revelation knowledge. Knowledge comes through the Word of God and revelation by the Holy Spirit.

The Holy Spirit gives revelation to the Word. Allow Him to reveal the Word of God to you, and you will have revelation knowledge.

Just as Elijah knew he could not complete his journey without obeying the angel of the Lord, we must realize that we cannot complete our walk with Him if we do not center upon Jesus. We must dine daily upon the Word of God as we allow the Holy Spirit to water our understanding.

## Strengthened to Move On

**And he arose, and did eat and drink, and went in the strength of that meat forty days and forty nights unto Horeb the mount of God.**

**1 Kings 19:8**

As Elijah ate and drank what was placed before him, he began to be strengthened. When he had received new strength, he got up and began to move. It is my belief that he did not ask God for direction, he just went.

When we eat of the Word and drink of the Holy Spirit, we need to inquire of God what He would have us to do.

When you come out of discouragement or depression, you need to stay close to God. Allow Him to feed you and strengthen you as you eat of His Word and drink of His

Spirit. Continue to ask Him for direction. He wants to give it to you.

The Holy Spirit will always lead us to God. But when we are coming out of discouragement, we may still make decisions based upon our feelings and not the leading of the Holy Spirit. In doing so, we may find ourselves in a dark place again. If this has happened to you, be assured that God has not given up on you.

Many times we make the wrong decision and do the wrong thing, yet we claim to have had a touch from God. We say, "I was discouraged, and I cried out. I was touched by God, and I even saw an angel. I began to eat of the Word and drink of the Holy Spirit. Then I received revelation knowledge, and I began to move out again, but I went the wrong direction."

Be comforted that even if you are going the wrong way, the Holy Spirit is not. God will not give up on you. He will continue to work with you until He gets you to the place He wants you to be. It just takes your staying in relationship with Him.

Now this does not mean that you can call out to God, stay in His Word and do anything you want. Elijah's heart *wanted* to get right with God. He had started on a path that was leading him in the wrong direction, and it had overcome his emotions and his mind. As a result, the angel of the Lord placed the bread and the water right beside his head. Elijah had to get that clear; he needed deliverance.

When Elijah began to get a little easing in his emotions, he got up and began to move again. But he did not ask God for direction.

My encouragement to you is this: If you have made a mistake, stay in touch with God. When He begins to move in you as you are in the Word and in prayer, ask for His direction instead of going ahead on your own with no divine guidance.

Just as that food and water strengthened Elijah so that he could go for forty days and forty nights, the Word of God and the Holy Spirit will also strengthen you.

You and I can move in the strength of the Word and the Holy Spirit, but we still need to have God's direction as to *where* He wants us to go in that strength.

## "What Are You Doing Here?"

> **And he came thither unto a cave, and lodged there; and, behold, the word of the Lord came to him, and he said unto him, What doest thou here, Elijah?**
>
> **1 Kings 19:9**

After coming to the mountain of Horeb, Elijah lodged in a cave there. He had gone in the wrong direction and had spent his strength, so he decided that this was where he was going to stay.

The cave in which Elijah lodged was a place of darkness, a place of separation, a place in which to hide once again. However, it is clear that Elijah still communed with God, because he heard His voice in his spirit. In his heart he heard God ask him, "Elijah, what are you doing back in the darkness, back in the kind of place I brought you out of?"

Despite his mistakes, God continued to work with Elijah. The discouragement that was in Elijah's heart is revealed in the next verse of Scripture.

## "I'm All Alone!"

> **And he said, I have been very jealous for the Lord God of hosts: for the children of Israel have forsaken thy covenant, thrown down thine altars, and slain thy prophets with the sword; and I, even I *only*, am left; and they seek my life, to take it away.**
>
> **1 Kings 19:10**

Discouragement says, "I'm all alone. I have failed, and I just want to die."

## Elijah: Discouragement From the Sayings of Others

Why did Elijah think he was alone?

Many people who are in discouragement cut themselves off from those who can help them. After they have cut *themselves* off, then they blame the very people they have rejected. They try to put the blame on someone else.

That is what Elijah did. He said, "I'm all alone. I'm the only one left. The Israelites have forsaken You, Lord, and now they're seeking to kill me. Nobody knows the troubles I've seen."

Once again Elijah falls back into self-pity.

Sometimes when we are coming out of discouragement and depression, there is a fight involved. When that happens, if we are not careful we will slip back into old habits, old conversations, old negative words.

Even though you may be involved in a fight, you plus God will win if you will continue to allow Him to work with you and in you. When you decide in your own strength where you will go, you will find yourself back in darkness again — back in that hiding place, that place of separation and despair. Don't just decide where you want to go; follow the Lord's direction and guidance.

## "Go Forth and Stand!"

And he said, Go forth, and stand upon the mount before the Lord.

**1 Kings 19:11**

When God asked Elijah, "What are you doing here?" Elijah tried to avoid the question by laying the blame for his actions on someone else. He said, "I'm all alone. Your people have forsaken You. I'm the only one left to serve You, and now the others are trying to kill me."

Then God spoke to Elijah and said, "Go forth, and stand on the mountain before Me."

When God spoke back to Elijah, notice that He didn't even acknowledge Elijah's negative response about the other people.

God doesn't want to hear about other people; He wants to hear about you and me. God definitely doesn't want to hear complaining, negativism, gossip or criticism.

Here in this passage, God is saying to us today the same thing He was saying to Elijah in his day, "All that may be so, but I'm still working with you, so get up and go forth!"

Notice that God told Elijah, "Go out and stand on the mountain before Me." There are many instances in the Word of God in which a mountain serves as a place of higher spiritual revelation. Jesus went up on the mountain to pray, and when He came down after a night of prayer, He appointed His twelve disciples. (Luke 6:12,13.) He had gone to the place of prayer to seek God, and He came down from that holy place with higher spiritual revelation.

Isaiah wrote, "How beautiful upon the mountains are the feet of him that bringeth good tidings..." (Is. 52:7). When we go to the mountain to pray, as we stand there with God, not only do we receive the lovely feet of those who bring good news, we also receive the revelation as to what we are to speak to the generation around us.

In the cave of darkness and despair, God spoke to Elijah and told him, "Go out and stand on the mountain before Me." In other words, the Lord was saying to Elijah, "Come, stand at a place where you can commune with Me. Come out of the darkness and into the light."

We can see how God moved Elijah. His purpose was to bring Elijah from the dark cave of separation back into the light of fellowship and communication with Him once again.

That is the drawing power of God. He will draw us toward the light. He will never depress our spirit, neutralize us, cut us off or stop us in any way by taking us into darkness. God doesn't want us to reside in dark places. He wants us out on the mountain top like the eagle, in the place of light.

## The Still Small Voice

> And, behold, the Lord passed by, and a great and strong wind rent the mountains, and brake in pieces the rocks before the Lord; but the Lord was not in the wind: and after the wind an earthquake; but the Lord was not in the earthquake:
>
> And after the earthquake a fire; but the Lord was not in the fire: and after the fire a still small voice.
> 1 Kings 19:11,12

This passage of Scripture shows us that God is not necessarily loud and boisterous. Being demonstrative is not necessarily a mark of power or a sign that God is in our midst. Being loud and boisterous doesn't mean that God is present. Being hushed and quiet doesn't mean that God is present. We do not determine God's presence by noise or by a lack of it. God comes however He determines, and we need to be able to recognize Him and His presence.

On some occasions, God will reveal Himself in mighty thundering, in fire, or in hail; but sometimes He speaks in a still quiet voice, like a gentle breeze.

I believe that when God wants to minister to us in our discouragement, we have to get to a place where we can hear Him. Going to the mountain of prayer and coming out into the light, we begin to hear that still small voice, that gentle moving of God upon our heart, our senses and emotions. God knows that we have need of kindly prodding at our time of discouragement.

So often what we do is seek the loud and boisterous, when we need the gentle moving. Then there are times when we seek the gentle moving or the still small voice, when what we need is a good dose of Holy Spirit shouting, praise and laughter unto God in order to be loosed from our bonds of discouragement and despair.

Emotionally, I believe that when we are discouraged we need to hear God for ourselves. We need to understand in our minds that Jesus is the *Bread of Life*. We need to partake of Him and to allow that thought to sizzle and burn on those hot stones of the Word of God. Then the watering that comes on the Word by the revelation of the Holy Spirit will bring forth the *rhema* — the personal word from God — that we need to deal with life's situations.

We need to listen for the voice of God, because when we give in to fear, we allow our emotions to clamor so loudly we become deaf to the Spirit. At times, the racket is so thunderous inside us that we can't hear anything, much less that *still small voice*. When we allow God to draw us by the Holy Spirit to our mountain of prayer, we will come out of darkness and confusion and into the light of His peaceful guidance.

That is the way God leads His mature sons and daughters, as we read in Romans 8:14. We are to be led by God through hearing His voice, the inner witness of the Holy Spirit.

## "What Are You Doing Here?"

**And it was so, when Elijah heard it, that he wrapped his face in his mantle, and went out, and stood in the entering in of the cave. And, behold, there came a voice unto him, and said, What doest thou here, Elijah?**
**1 Kings 19:13**

When God begins to draw us, He will draw us to the place where we can hear Him again.

When Elijah heard the still small voice, what did He do? He wrapped his face in his mantle, went out and stood in the entrance of the cave. There, once again, he heard the voice of the Lord say to him, "Elijah, what are you doing here?"

Sometimes when we hear the voice of God, we don't always do the correct thing. Sometimes when God touches us, we don't always respond as we should. Does this mean that we should become discouraged again? Does it mean that we should give up or that we should quit? Absolutely not! We should never give up.

If you don't give up, God can continue to work in your life. So don't give up on God, because He will never give up on you.

What was the first thing that Elijah did when he heard the voice of God? He wrapped himself in his mantle. A mantle can be thought of as a cloak of protection; it can also be thought of as a cloak of calling.

When you hear God calling you, never cover yourself with your own protective devices. God wants you to open yourself up and come to Him.

Too often today we have a tendency to ignore the voice of God. When God says to us, "Come on out farther into the entrance of the light, it is not going to blind you; come on out," we begin to cover ourselves with the mantle of our calling. We begin to go to God as pastor, as evangelist, as prophet, as apostle, as teacher, in our mantle of calling. God wants us to come to Him not as His dutiful servants but as His beloved children.

When we are in emotional situations, we cannot hide behind our protective devices. We must strip ourselves and go before God saying, "Here am I, Lord. I lay down my calling and stand before You just as I am. I am discouraged, and I need Your help."

When Elijah went out to the entrance of the cave, he was on the edge of darkness and yet on the edge of light.

When you find yourself on the edge between darkness and light, you will see that the light of God that is drawing you out is much more powerful than the power of darkness that is drawing you back in. If you will keep your eyes on God, He will continue to call you out of darkness and into light, out of discouragement and defeat and into joy and victory.

As Elijah stood there, the voice of the Lord came to him and asked him once again, "Elijah, what are you doing here?"

The Lord is asking you and me the same thing He asked Elijah. He wants us to look at where we are and decide where we are going from here. We need to learn from our mistakes. We must learn not to dwell on the past, but to keep our eyes on the future.

One of the best ways I have learned to hear the voice of God is by looking at my own actions, whether in my personal life or in the gifts of the Spirit, judging them and learning from them, as well as from the victories I have enjoyed. Although I don't dwell on past failures, I do benefit from them.

So once more God asked Elijah, "What are you doing here?" The Lord wanted Elijah to understand that He was the One Who had touched him. He wanted Elijah to know that he could not go on in his own power, but that he needed God's divine strength.

You and I are not to go forth in our own power, but in the strength of the Lord. We are not to go just anywhere we want to go. We are to take the Word of God, be filled with His Spirit, receive His direction and go forth, walking in the light that He sheds on our way — right into heaven.

## "I'm the Only One Left!"

**And he said, I have been very jealous for the Lord God of hosts: because the children of Israel have**

forsaken thy covenant, thrown down thine altars, and slain thy prophets with the sword; and I, even I *only*, am left; and they seek my life, to take it away.
                                      1 Kings 19:14

This was exactly the same thing that Elijah had answered the Lord in verse 10: "Lord, Your people have all turned against You and have torn down Your altars and killed Your prophets; I'm the only one left!"

However, this time I believe that Elijah spoke it with less conviction because he had received more light than he had before.

After Elijah had spoken these words, in the following verses the Lord responded to him and gave him some new instructions as to where he was to go and what he was to do.

## "I Have Seven Thousand Elijahs!"

And the Lord said unto him, Go, return on thy way to the wilderness of Damascus: and when thou comest, anoint Hazael to be king over Syria:

And Jehu the son of Nimshi shalt thou anoint to be king over Israel: and Elisha the son of Shaphat of Abelmeholah shalt thou anoint to be prophet in thy room.

And it shall come to pass, that him that escapeth the sword of Hazael shall Jehu slay: and him that escapeth from the sword of Jehu shall Elisha slay.

Yet I have left me seven thousand in Israel, all the knees which have not bowed unto Baal, and every mouth which hath not kissed him.
                                   1 Kings 19:15-18

In these verses the Lord was saying, in essence, "Elijah, now that you have been drawn out of the darkness and into the light and I have your full attention, I have something to tell you. Your call has not left you, because My call is without repentance. This is what I want you to do."

*Say Good-bye to Discouragement!*

The Lord ignored Elijah's whining and complaining and dealt with him about his call. He sent him to anoint kings over Syria and Israel, and to anoint Elisha to succeed him as prophet. Now that he had come out into the light, Elijah was once again receiving the direction, instruction and revelation from God that he needed to walk into the future.

To reassure him, the Lord ended by telling Elijah that He had reserved seven thousand who, like him, had not bowed their knee to Baal or worshipped his image.

In his fear and flight, in his discouragement and despair, Elijah had made a big mistake. He had thought that he was the only person in the whole kingdom who was left to serve the Lord. But God said to him, "Elijah, you were *never* alone. You were always surrounded by those who *could* have and *would* have helped you. You lost sight of that fact because you *listened to the messenger of fear.*"

If you are discouraged today, if you have been depressed and have cut yourself off from your minister or those who can help you, those whom God has sent to surround you and uplift you, it is time to do what Elijah did — turn around and go the other way.

I encourage you to take the first step today. Call a godly, spiritual friend from whom you have separated yourself. Go back to church. Come out of the cave, out of the darkness. As you begin to walk into the light, the Spirit of the Lord will lead you to those you need and to those who need you.

God has victory for you just as He did for Elijah. If you will listen to Him, He will lead you step by step to fulfill your calling, your ministry and your walk with Jesus Christ in victory.

# 3
# Moses: Discouragement From the Burden of Responsibility

In this chapter we are going to look at Moses, a man who became discouraged because of the burdens of responsibility and the pressures that came to bear upon him because of that responsibility.

Now I would like to remind you, right off, that the Lord has assured us in His Word that His yoke is easy and His burden is light. (Matt. 11:30.) When our burdens become so heavy that we cannot carry them or stand up under them, that is a sign that something is wrong. Somewhere, somehow, we have left open a door to the enemy to come in and cause problems for us.

Moses, like every human being (including us today!) was subject to the pressures of responsibility and the burden that accompanies it. In order to examine his situation and learn from it, we must also consider those people who surrounded him, because no one ever bears responsibility alone. There are always those who influence us in our decisions and actions.

Let's look at Moses and his environment to see the things he did correctly and the things he did incorrectly and then learn from his example.

## The People Complained

*Now the people became like those who complain of adversity in the hearing of the Lord; and when the*

Lord heard it, His anger was kindled, and the fire of the Lord burned among them and consumed some of the outskirts of the camp.

**Numbers 11:1 NAS**

When this verse says that the Children of Israel, whom Moses was leading out of bondage in Egypt, "became like those who complain of adversity," it does not specify who "those" were. But as we travel down through the Scriptures, we will discover their identity.

Here we are told simply that the Children of Israel had become like others among them, just as we sometimes do. Like us, they had begun to conform to their surroundings, to be pressured into being like the world around them. They had begun to become like the people who were found on all sides of them. Instead of being an example to others, the Children of Israel had begun to be influenced by their neighbors, by "those who complain of adversity."

If we are not careful, we will do the same thing. That's why we need to surround ourselves with people who are positive and upbeat, people who are in the Word of God, those who encourage us and do not discourage us, those who build us up and do not tear us down.

In our life and ministry we deal with a variety of people, individuals of all different types, and that's wonderful. But we have to be careful to whom we listen, because people do have an influence upon us and our attitude and actions.

## In the Hearing of God

Notice that not only did these people complain of adversity, but they did it "in the hearing of the Lord." In Psalm 78:19 we read that these people spoke against God openly. Not only did they complain against God, but they also complained against God's man. They were in open rebellion.

Now we have seen that discouraged people are often negative people. That's why we must guard against becoming discouraged and disheartened. Because we are going to run into adverse circumstances in every stage of life, we must determine now how we are going to react to these adverse situations.

In Colossians 3:2 NAS we are told by the Apostle Paul, "Set your mind on the things above, not on the things that are on earth." When the Bible says "set your mind," it means "get an attitude." So we need to develop a good attitude. We need to determine that, come what may, we are going to set our mind on things above and not on things below.

In this life we are going to encounter adverse circumstances. Jesus called them tribulations. (John 16:33.) If we set our mind on these things from below, then we are always going to be complaining, and complaining leads to discouragement, for us and for everyone around us. But if we set our mind on things above, if we develop a right and positive attitude, we will look to the promises of God. We will look past the adversities of life to the victory that is ours in Jesus. Not only will we be encouraged, we will encourage all those around us.

We are supposed to set our mind on things, but we are supposed to set it on the right things, and those are the things that are above.

If you want to be able to overcome adversities, the tribulations that you will encounter in this life, set your mind on things above. Develop a good, right and positive attitude. It will do wonders for you and for everyone around you.

## God Heard It and Acted

Finally, notice that when these people complained, God heard their complaint.

That means that when you and I complain, God hears us too. God knows exactly what is going on in our lives. He sees and hears how we handle it.

What did God do when He heard these people complaining? His anger was kindled against them, and He sent a fire that burned among them and consumed some of them on the edge of their camp.

What happened then?

## And Moses Interceded

**The people therefore cried out to Moses, and Moses prayed to the Lord, and the fire died out.**
**Numbers 11:2 NAS**

Here we see Moses doing just what God wanted him to do — intercede for those in his care.

When these people began to complain so much that they angered the Lord and brought His wrath down upon themselves, who did they run to? They ran to the man of God, the very person they had been complaining about, the person they were in open rebellion against.

This happens so often. God gives us responsibility over families, churches and ministries, and many times the people in our charge do nothing but complain about our leadership. Every time some situation arises that they don't like, they go into rebellion against us. Yet when trouble comes, when they find themselves in a situation they can't handle, where do they turn? They turn to the godly person who is shouldering the responsibility for them.

So these people ran to Moses. What did the man of God do? He prayed. He made intercession for the people for whom he bore responsibility.

This is the mark of a man or woman of God — the ability to carry a heavy responsibility without becoming discouraged. But constant complaining can eventually wear down even a man or woman of God.

In time, complaining people can wear down even the strongest of us. That's what happened to Moses. In every situation they encountered on the way from Egypt to the Promised Land, he prayed for the people. He interceded for them with God, just as he prayed for them here and the fire of God's anger went out.

Do you pray? Do you intercede for those in your charge, those for whom you bear godly responsibility?

## The Rabble Are Roused

So the name of that place was called Taberah, because the fire of the Lord burned among them.

And the rabble who were among them had greedy desires.

Numbers 11:3,4 NAS

Now we see who "those" were in verse 1. They were the "rabble" among the Hebrew tribes. These were the people whom the Children of Israel became like.

We read about these people in Exodus 12:38 NAS which says that when the Hebrews left Egypt, "...a mixed multitude also went up with them, along with flocks and herds, a very large number of livestock." This mixed multitude of people were probably slaves.

Jamieson, Fausset and Brown's commentary on the whole Bible says that this mixed multitude consisted of Egyptians.[1] Matthew Henry's commentary says that they came with the Children of Israel out of Egypt, "expecting only the land of promise, but not a state of probation in the way to it. These were the scabbed sheep that infected the flock, the leaven that leavened the whole lump."[2]

---

[1] Robert Jamieson, A. R. Fausset, and David Brown, *Commentary Practical and Explanatory on the Whole Bible* (Grand Rapids, MI: Zondervan Publishing House, 1961, 1978), p. 119.

[2] Matthew Henry, *Commentary on the Whole Bible* (Grand Rapids, MI: Regency Reference Library, an imprint of Zondervan Publishing House, 1960), p. 152.

*The New Bible Commentary Revised* states that the mixed multitude were "the rabble," or "the 'riff-raff', as the word has been translated."[3] Dake's commentary says that "the mixed multitude...would be the descendants of the original servants of Abraham, Isaac and Jacob besides a few Egyptians who had married Israelites."[4]

So there are different opinions as to exactly who the mixed multitude were, but the one thing that we do know is that they were the rabble, the riff-raff, those who had "greedy desires," or as the *King James Version* says, those who "fell a lusting."

These are people who came out of Egypt at the same time as the nation of Israel. You will remember that when God brought His people out of bondage in Egypt, according to the psalmist, "He brought them forth also with silver and gold: and there was not one feeble person among their tribes" (Ps. 105:37).

God had done great things for the Children of Israel. He had worked mighty signs and wonders on their behalf. He had provided for them and taken care of them. He had caused them to come forth from among the Egyptians strong in body and laden down with treasure. The mixed multitude, the rabble, the riff-raff who came with them, thought this was a good deal — and they wanted in on it.

These people were not committed to God. They were only committed to getting in on the promises given to God's people. They were not interested in the work of the Lord, only the benefits of it. Right away they began to manifest their "greedy desires." They "fell a lusting" — but after the things below, not the things above.

---

[3] D. Guthrie and J. A. Motyer, editors; A. M. Stibbs and D. J. Wiseman, consulting editors, *The New Bible Commentary Revised* (Grand Rapids, MI: Wm. B. Eerdmans Publishing Co., copyright 1970 by Inter-Varsity Press, London), p. 180.

[4] Finis Jennings Dake, *Dake's Annotated Reference Bible* (Lawrenceville, GA: Dake Bible Sales, Inc., 1961), p. 168.

## "What Shall We Eat?"

*...and also the sons of Israel wept again and said, "Who will give us meat to eat?"*

**Numbers 11:4 NAS**

Even though the man of God had prayed for the Israelites (as we saw in verse 2) to get them out of the trouble they were in (as described in verse 1) because they were in open rebellion against God and God's man, they turned right around and listened once again to these same people — this rabble, this mixed multitude, this riff-raff.

Now I must warn you that in the Church of Jesus Christ there are among us those who are not truly committed to God or to His people or to His work. They are not committed to seeing the plan of God proceed and come to its final culmination. They are only committed to reaping the benefits that come on God's people. They see the healings, the deliverances, the provision, the safety and security of God's people, and they want to get in on the blessings — but they don't want to be committed to God and to the fulfillment of the vision.

We in the Body of Christ have got to grow up. We must learn to spot these people. We must be careful not to listen to them. We must not conform ourselves to their ideas, because they are negative, discouraged, complaining, greedy people. If we are not watchful, their negativism, discouragement, unhappiness and greediness will rub off on us and make us the same way.

Unless we are on our guard, such people will cause discouragement to come not only upon us, but also upon those who exercise spiritual authority and responsibility over us, which is what happened to Moses.

Instead of lining up with those who were committed to seeing God's plan brought forth to completion, the Israelites lined up with the rabble among them. They listened to the riff-raff in their midst and conformed themselves to them.

As we have seen, discouragement will cause people to conform to their surroundings. The people of God, the nation of Israel, lost their godly form and began to take on the form of those around them. They started to think, talk and act like the rabble who had "greedy desires," those who "fell a lusting," those whose eyes were on the things below rather than on the things above. And one of those things was *meat*.

In the *King James Version* of Numbers 11:4 the word *meat* is translated "flesh." So the people were saying, "Who is going to give us flesh?"

The spiritual parallel is obvious. As we have noted, today in the Church of Jesus Christ there are those who have no commitment to the goals and visions of God but who are only committed to satisfying the demands and desires of the flesh.

## "We Remember the Good Old Days!"

> "We remember the fish which we used to eat free in Egypt, the cucumbers and the melons and the leeks and the onions and the garlic."
>
> **Numbers 11:5 NAS**

Notice that the very next thing these people say is, "We remember."

When you begin to associate and identify with those who complain, those who have greedy desires, you will begin to remember the things of the past. All of a sudden the past will begin to look very good to you. It will become romantic and appealing in comparison to the present or even the future.

These people said, "We remember the fish we used to eat free in Egypt." Now they were not remembering correctly, because they did not eat anything free in Egypt. They were slaves to the Egyptians. They had to work from before sunup to after sundown. Every ounce they ate or drank, whether it was vegetables, bread, water or fish, they paid for with a pound of hard labor. They received nothing free in Egypt. Yet they remembered the fish they used to eat "free" there.

Then they went on to recall "the cucumbers, the melons, the leeks and the onions and the garlic." Most biblical teachers see Egypt as a type and shadow of the world. God delivered the nation of Israel out of the kingdom of Egypt, the king being Pharaoh, in the same way that Jesus Christ came to this earth and delivered us out of the world, whose ruler is Satan.

So Egypt is a type and shadow of the world, and Pharaoh is as a type and shadow of Satan.

Like the Children of Israel who began to listen to the wrong people and to look back to the "fleshpots" of Egypt, today many in the Church of Jesus Christ are listening to the wrong people and are looking back to the pleasures and enticements of the world.

Just as the Israelites received nothing free in Egypt, we Christians receive nothing free in this world. Everything has a price tag.

These people were recalling not only the "free" fish, but also the cucumbers and leeks, the onions and the garlic they had enjoyed in Egypt. All these things I call "little stinkers." That's what such people themselves become — "little stinkers" — those who go "a lusting" after the spice of life rather than seeking the Bread of Life.

## Fleshly Food or Spiritual Food?

"But now our appetite is gone. There is nothing at all to look at except this manna."
**Numbers 11:6 NAS**

We know that manna, "the bread of heaven" as it is called in Psalm 105:40, is a symbol of God's provision. To these people, that was not enough. Instead of feeding on the spiritual bread of life, they preferred to feed on that which would satisfy their flesh.

That is exactly what is happening in many of our churches today.

I often hear people say things like, "I would go to that church, but it is just a teaching center." That is what a church is supposed to be. A church is to be a place where the fivefold ministry equips and prepares and trains the Body of Christ to go out into the world and do the work of service. (Eph. 4:11-15.) It is a place where "the bread of heaven," the manna, God's provision, is handed out so that His people may be built up and encouraged. It is not a place where the flesh is pandered to, but a place where the spirit is provided for.

## Moses Heard and Was Displeased

**Now Moses heard the people weeping throughout their families, each man at the doorway of his tent; and the anger of the Lord was kindled greatly, and Moses was displeased.**

**Numbers 11:10 NAS**

Verses 7 through 9 describe the manna, the "bread of heaven," God's provision. Then here in verse 10 we get back to the story. In this verse we are told the reason Moses began to slide into discouragement.

Notice the first three words: "And Moses *heard*...." The mistake that Moses made was giving these people his ear. He began paying attention to their weeping, their desire to have their flesh pandered to. As a result, just like those to whom he was listening, he became displeased, which is one of the first steps toward discouragement.

When people in positions of godly authority and responsibility turn their eyes and ears from the Word of God, away from "the bread of heaven," to the demands and desires of the people to satisfy their flesh, they will inevitably begin to slide toward discouragement.

The *King James Version* of this verse says that "Moses heard the people *weep*." According to the concordance, the Hebrew word translated *weep* in this context means generally "to bemoan" or to "complain."[5] In another context, the Hebrew word translated *bemoan* means to "waver," "be sorry" or "deplore."[6]

Although it is good to listen to other people and give them our full attention, we must not make the mistake of trying to pander to their flesh. Dissatisfied, grumbling, self-pitying, complaining people are fleshly people. If we are not careful, they will wear us out.

That is what happened to Moses.

The Bible says that Moses listened to these people complaining "throughout their families." They made this spiritual affair into a family affair. They began to complain about the man of God in their homes. Just as many in the Church do today, they had the man of God "for lunch" — not by inviting him to their home for a meal, but by roasting him over their family fire!

If you have a complaint about a man or woman of God, I encourage you not to take it to your family, but first talk to God to determine whether it is just you and your problem. If necessary, then take it directly to the person involved. In the home, don't get into a discussion in front of your children about the man or woman of God who has spiritual authority and responsibility over you. If you do, it will cause your children to develop a disregard and disrespect for those who have spiritual authority and responsibility

---

[5]James Strong, *Strong's Exhaustive Concordance of the Bible* (Nashville: Abingdon, 1890), "Hebrew and Chaldee Dictionary," p. 21, entry #1058.

[6]Strong, p. 77, entry #5110.

over them. You will be sowing the seeds of rebellion not only against the leaders of the church, but also against the One Who chose and anointed and commissioned them — just as these people were doing when they complained about Moses, which is what angered the Lord.

Moses heard each one of these people complaining "at the doorway of his tent." This simply means that not only were they complaining in their homes and families, but they were also complaining in public where anyone and everyone could see and hear.

That too is dangerous business.

As a result, not only was the anger of the Lord "greatly kindled," but Moses himself was "displeased." Both God and Moses knew that he was being talked about. Moses was aware that those in his charge were not happy with him, and that knowledge began to make him unhappy too. He became displeased, which, as we have said, is the first sign of discouragement. The reason he was so displeased and discouraged was because he was physically and emotionally beaten down by their constant "weeping" — their continual griping and complaining.

There is a pattern here. *First* Moses was beaten down by the people's continual griping and complaining. *Then* he became unhappy. He listened instead of guarding his heart.

## Moses Begins to Complain

**So Moses said to the Lord, "Why hast Thou been so hard on Thy servant? And why have I not found favor in Thy sight, that Thou hast laid the burden of all this people on me?"**

**Numbers 11:11 NAS**

Once again we see that Moses began to become displeased and discouraged because of the burden of his responsibility for the people. So he began to accuse God of causing all his troubles. He began to look upon the call of God as an affliction rather than a blessing. He didn't blame the people, and he didn't blame himself; rather, he blamed God.

"Why," he asked the Lord, "have You laid the burden of all these people on *me*?"

Does that complaint remind you of anything that Elijah the prophet said to the Lord? "I am so miserable because *I* am the only one left to worship and serve You!"

When those of us in the ministry become discouraged, often we do just what Elijah and Moses did. We complain to the Lord because we no longer enjoy our ministry. We no longer find it a joy to minister to God's people, to fulfill His dream and vision.

When you and I become "weary in well doing" (2 Thess. 3:13), often we begin to blame God because we think He is treating us unfairly. We accuse Him of putting an affliction on us, rather than thanking and praising Him for blessing us.

That is a mark of discouragement.

## "How Will I Meet Their Demands?"

> "Was it I who conceived all this people? Was it I who brought them forth, that Thou shouldest say to me, 'Carry them in your bosom as a nurse carries a nursing infant, to the land which Thou didst swear to their fathers?'
>
> "Where am I to get meat to give to all this people? For they weep before me, saying, 'Give us meat that we may eat!'"
>
> Numbers 11:12,13 NAS

Here we see Moses as a man overwhelmed with his ministry. The reason he was overwhelmed is because he had begun to listen to people who were weeping and complaining. He got into discouragement by trying to meet their demands.

In his frustration and discouragement, he asked the Lord, "How am I going to meet the demands of the people for meat? Where am I going to get what they ask for to satisfy the desires of their flesh?"

As men and women of God, we are not called to meet the demands of people who only seek to have their fleshly desires pandered to. We are called, in any responsibility that is ours, to walk according to the Word of God and the leading of the Holy Spirit. We are not here to give people what they want but to give them "the bread of life." If we try to do otherwise, we will end up in frustration and discouragement like Moses.

## "I Just Want To Die!"

"I alone am not able to carry all this people, because it is too burdensome for me.

"So if Thou art going to deal thus with me, please kill me at once, if I have found favor in Thy sight, and do not let me see my wretchedness."

Numbers 11:14,15 NAS

Here we see the same attitudes in Moses that were in Elijah when he fell into discouragement after running away in fear from Jezebel and her threats.

In verse 14 Moses says, "I alone...." Like Elijah, he claims to be the only one in his situation. He feels sorry for himself because he feels that the burden the Lord has given him is just too heavy for him to bear.

Then in verse 15 he prays, "Please kill me at once." Now, as we said when we studied Elijah's situation, God is not in the killing business. He is not in the business of discouraging us, of pushing us down and depressing us. On the contrary, God is in the business of encouraging us, of lifting us up so we can go forth to do our work for Him.

When Moses asked God to kill him immediately, he was simply expressing a desire for escape. This escapist attitude is typical of those who fall into discouragement, but it is not God's answer to the problem, as we see in His response to Moses' request.

## "Call for the Elders"

**The Lord therefore said to Moses, "Gather for Me seventy men from the elders of Israel, whom you know to be the elders of the people and their officers and bring them to the tent of meeting, and let them take their stand there with you."**

**Numbers 11:16 NAS**

Just as with Elijah, God didn't answer this negative talk. Instead, He dealt with Moses according to what He wanted *him* to do.

Although Moses was in discouragement, his heart was still open to God. So the Lord answered him and gave him some directions about what to do to solve his problem. He told him to call together seventy elders of the people and bring them with him to the meeting place.

Although the word elder means old, I do not think these were people who were simply advanced in age. These people may have been old in years, but the reason they were chosen was not just because of their long life, but because of their spiritual maturity.

Elders are not just those who have gray hair, but those who have a long-standing, mature relationship with the Lord. That is the kind of people we need to help us in our ministry, those who are mature in their knowledge of God and in their devotion to His work, those who have proven themselves committed to the cause of Christ.

So the first part of God's answer for Moses' problem was to choose those whom he knew to be elders among the people.

## "The Burden Will Be Shared"

> "Then I will come down and speak with you there, and I will take of the Spirit who is upon you and will put Him upon them; and they shall bear the burden of the people with you, so that you shall not bear it all alone."
>
> **Numbers 11:17 NAS**

The Lord told Moses to call these people together in the tent of meeting. There He would anoint them with the Holy Spirit as He did Moses, and they would share the burden among them.

God already had a plan to lighten Moses' burden so he could be better able to bear it.

God always has a plan for every situation and need we may face in life. He always has directions and instructions for us, just as He did for Moses. He doesn't want our burden to be heavy. He has told us already that His yoke is easy and His burden is light. (Matt. 11:30).

If our burden becomes so heavy that we cannot carry it, then something is wrong. We need to go to the Lord and seek His answer for how to make that burden (as His burden is) lighter and easier to bear.

That's what He was doing with Moses when He told him to call for the elders of the people so He could divide the burden among them.

## The Cord of Three Strands

Notice that in verse 16 the Lord told Moses to choose seventy men, people whom he *knew* to be elders of the people. These were to be those who were in agreement with Moses and his mission and ministry.

When we go forth to choose those who will help us shoulder our burden of responsibility, we must first choose "elders," those who have a long-term relationship with God. Then we must choose those whom we "know," those who have a close relationship with us. Finally, we must choose those who are known "of the people," those who have a relationship with the people who will be in their charge.

Those chosen must be mature, tried and true in their relationship with the Lord. Then they must be in full agreement with the mission and ministry of the one alongside whom they will stand. And finally, they must be known and trusted by those who will rely upon them.

The Lord told Moses to bring those he had chosen to "the tent of meeting," that is, the church. Likewise, those whom we choose as elders must be people who are faithful in their church attendance and service.

Finally, the Lord told Moses, "Once the elders are chosen and brought to the tent of meeting, let them take their stand with you." This means that these people must be willing to stand alongside the one who chooses them. They must be ready and able to take their place, to fulfill their station or position beside their leader.

In Ecclesiastes 4:12 we read that a cord of three strands is not easily broken. When you have people of these three "strands" — strength in their commitment to God, to you and to the people — then you can be sure that the bond you form together with them cannot be easily broken.

When you follow this God-ordained criterion for choosing the people who are going to be standing with you in faith and service, you can be assured that with God's help you will succeed in your ministry to the Lord and to others.

This criterion is also true for your business, household or any organization in which you have responsibility.

## "Stop, Look and Listen!"

The Lord promised Moses that if he would call together the elders of the people, He would take of the Spirit that was upon him and place it upon the seventy chosen to assist him. Then he would not have to bear the burden of responsibility for the people by himself.

What the Lord was promising was that the Holy Spirit would come down upon them. Why? Because it takes the Holy Spirit to fulfill the vision and to carry out the responsibility of ministry.

The Lord was telling Moses, "If you will find the right people, those who will be faithful and obedient to follow My directions, I will see to it that they have the same spirit that you have."

God was telling Moses the same thing He told Elijah: "You were never alone. These people were there all the time."

But when Moses looked, what he saw was based on what he was hearing, and all he was hearing were complaints. These people were not complaining, so he couldn't see them or hear them. These are the ones he should have been looking for and listening for. They were the ones who would help him carry the burden of responsibility for the people.

Although these people were always there, Moses never saw them or heard them because he had his eyes and ears trained on the complainers in their midst. As long as he paid attention to them, he missed seeing and hearing what God wanted him to see and hear. Therefore, he went into discouragement and despondency, which leads to depression and despair.

Don't make the same mistake that Moses made. When God tells you to do something — whether it is to take responsibility for a church, a ministry, an evangelistic association, a company, a Bible study, a family or a relationship — be assured He will send you the people you need to stand with you and help you to fulfill the vision He has placed in your heart.

Remember, you are never alone. But you do need to look at and listen to the people who are surrounding you, the people in your own vicinity, those in your own sphere of influence. Because the ones whom God has chosen to help you are usually there with you, right where you are.

## "Give Me Wisdom and Knowledge!"

In the night God appeared to Solomon, and said to him, "Ask what I shall give you."

And Solomon said to God, "Thou hast dealt with my father David with great loving-kindness, and hast made me king in his place.

"Now, O Lord God, Thy promise to my father David is fulfilled; for Thou hast made me king over a people as numerous as the dust of the earth.

"Give me now wisdom and knowledge, that I may go out and come in before this people; for who can rule this great people of Thine?"

2 Chronicles 1:7-10 NAS

Don't give up. Don't bail out. Don't cry out to God that you want to die. Don't try to escape from responsibility by saying, "Let somebody else do it, I'm just not able. All I want to do is be left alone." Instead, do what King Solomon did. Go to God and ask Him for the wisdom and knowledge, the strength and direction you need to carry the burden of responsibility that He has placed upon you.

In Judges 13:2-8 we read that when Manoah's wife was told by an angel that she would conceive and give birth to a child who would be named Samson, Manoah prayed and asked the Lord to send a man of God to teach them how to raise the child they had been promised.

Like Solomon and Manoah and his wife, each of us has been given responsibility. Our responsibility may not be over a kingdom or even over a mighty man of God, but we are responsible in every area of our own life. If we will go to

Him, the Lord will provide the answers and directions we need to carry out those responsibilities in accordance with His divine will and plan.

When Moses went before the Lord complaining about the burden of his responsibility, God gave him a simple solution: "Delegate authority."

## "Get Rid of What's Weighing You Down!"

The Lord told Moses, in essence, "Get rid of what is weighing you down."

Each of us must go before the Lord and learn exactly what it is that is weighing us down. With Moses it was a wrong attitude and outlook brought about by listening to the wrong people.

If you will ask Him to do so, the Lord will point out to you what is weighing you down and will give you directions on what to do to get rid of it.

In Psalm 55:22 NAS, the psalmist says, "Cast your burden upon the Lord, and He will sustain you; He will never allow the righteous to be shaken." This verse lines up with 1 Peter 5:7, which tells us to cast all our cares upon the Lord because He cares for us.

Every time cares, worries, anxieties and burdens begin to weigh down upon you, practice casting them upon the Lord. Don't take them on, and don't embrace them. Cast them away! Give them to the Lord, because He has promised to sustain you. If you embrace them, if you hold fast to them, then God cannot sustain you, because your trust is not in Him but in yourself, in your ability to handle the situation on your own.

In Psalm 46:10 NAS the Lord says, "'Cease striving and know that I am God....'" In the annotated version, the side rendering for "cease striving" is "let go, relax."[7] What the Lord is saying to you here in this passage is, "Cease striving, let go, relax and know that I am God."

Let me reiterate, when discouragement comes and complains to you, take those complaints to God. Give your feelings to the Lord. Don't allow them to fester in you but take them to the One Who has the solution to your situation and need. He will tell you what to do.

Don't let those festering feelings cause you to be neutralized, to be conformed and pressured into the world's mold.

Don't allow complaining people to beat you down, wear you down or break you down. That was the mistake that Moses made. Call upon those you know to be strong — strong in their relationship with God, in their relationship with you and in their relationship with the people. Call upon them and let them stand with you. Believe that God is going to do something in you and in them.

Finally, cast all your cares upon the Lord. Roll them over onto Him. Let Him take the pressure of all those burdens and responsibilities.

Cease striving. Let go, relax and let God be God in your life. He doesn't want you beaten down, worn down or broken down. He doesn't want you discouraged, despondent or depressed. He is saying to you, "Get up and start again. I've got the answer for you!"

---

[7] *New American Standard Bible* (Nashville: Thomas Nelson Publishers, 1990), reference notes, p. 638.

# 4
# Reuben and Gad: Discouragement From Settling for the Suitable

As we have seen thus far, discouragement can come from fear and from the burden of responsibility. Another cause of discouragement can be settling for the suitable instead of pressing on to receive the fulfillment of the promise. Often, settling for the suitable is also the result of listening to the sayings of others rather than listening to the Word of the Lord.

Remember that it was the sayings of the evil queen Jezebel that caused Elijah to become discouraged, and it was listening to the sayings of the people that caused Moses to become discouraged. Now let's look at how listening to the sayings of others affected the Children of Israel when it came time to claim their inheritance from the Lord.

The story begins when the Israelites reached the Jordan River across from Canaan for the second time. There, Moses spoke to them and reminded them of what had happened to them the first time they had come to the border of the Promised Land forty years before.

## "The Land Is Yours!"

"And I said to you, 'You have come to the hill country of the Amorites which the Lord our God is about to give us.

'See, the Lord your God has placed the land before you; go up, take possession, as the Lord, the God of your fathers, has spoken to you. Do not fear or be dismayed.'

> "Then all of you approached me and said, 'Let us send men before us, that they may search the land for us, and bring back to us word of the way by which we should go up, and the cities which we shall enter'....
>
> "Yet you were not willing to go up, but rebelled against the command of the Lord your God;
>
> and you grumbled in your tents and said, 'Because the Lord hates us, He has brought us out of the land of Egypt to deliver us into the hand of the Amorites to destroy us.
>
> 'Where can we go up? Our brethren have made our hearts melt, saying, "The people are bigger and taller than we; the cities are large and fortified to heaven. And besides, we saw the sons of the Anakim there."'"
>
> **Deuteronomy 1:20-22,26-28 NAS**

Notice that statement, "Our brethren have made our hearts *melt* by saying...." Remember that one of the definitions of the phrase "to discourage" which we looked at in Chapter 1 was to melt. We said that when people's hearts melt, they begin to be pressured to conform to their surroundings.

Notice also what caused the hearts of the people to melt. It was the *sayings* of their brethren who had scouted out the land promised them by God. What did these scouts say? "The people are bigger than we; the cities are large and fortified to heaven. And besides we saw the Anakim there."

The Anakim were giants. So the Israelites were afraid to go in and take possession of their rightful inheritance because of the *sayings* that there were giants in the land.

What was Moses' response to their fear? Let's read it in his own words.

## "You Did Not Trust the Lord!"

> "Then I said to you, 'Do not be shocked, nor fear them.

'The Lord your God who goes before you will Himself fight on your behalf, just as He did for you in Egypt before your eyes,

and in the wilderness where you saw how the Lord your God carried you, just as a man carries his son, in all the way which you have walked, until you came to this place.'

"But for all this, you did not trust the Lord your God."

**Numbers 2:29-32 NAS**

Again we see how the sayings of others can melt the hearts of a whole nation and cause them to become discouraged, even though the Lord their God had brought them out of bondage in Egypt by many miracles, signs and wonders done by His mighty hand. As a result of their fear and discouragement, they were turned away from the land of promise and were forced to wander in the wilderness for forty years.

Now, forty years later, this nation had once again come to the borders of the Promised Land. To see how they responded this time, let's look at Chapter 32 of the book of Numbers.

## Don't Settle for the Suitable!

**Now the sons of Reuben and the sons of Gad had an exceedingly large number of livestock. So when they saw the land of Jazer and the land of Gilead [to the east of the Jordan River], that it was indeed a place suitable for livestock....**

**Numbers 32:1 NAS**

One of the things that these sons of Reuben and Gad had in common with the Israelites who were sent in to spy out the Promised Land was that they were both ruled by their senses. Both groups saw something and were affected by what they saw. The spies saw giants in the land. The sons of Reuben and Gad saw "a place suitable for livestock."

The *King James Version* says that "the place was a place for cattle," meaning that it was a place suitable for the purpose of these two tribes, which was to locate grazing lands for their huge herds of livestock.

When they saw this place on the eastern bank of the Jordan River, they were ruled by their senses rather than by the commandment of the Lord to press on to receive the fulfillment of the promise. In this, they were like the spies who had been ruled by their senses and had given in to fear rather than pressing on to take possession of the Promised Land.

When the sons of Reuben and Gad saw the land that was suitable for livestock, they wanted to stop. God has never called us to settle for the suitable. Rather, He has called us to press on toward what He has promised us.

Any time we set out to fulfill the promise of God, we will have opportunities to settle for the suitable. But as children of God, as joint heirs with Jesus Christ, we do not have to settle for what our senses tell us is suitable. One of the greatest enemies of the attainment of the promises of God is the "suitable." Most of us want to settle, instead of pushing on to receive God's best for us — which is what we can and should do.

In Galatians 6:9 the Apostle Paul wrote, "...let us not be weary in well doing: for in due season we shall reap, if we faint not."

There is a "due season" for each of us. Therefore, never, ever settle for the suitable. Don't give up. Don't quit. Don't stop short. Don't settle for the suitable, but press on until you receive the complete fulfillment of the promise of God.

## They Came, Saying....

**The sons of Gad and the sons of Reuben came and spoke to Moses and to Eleazar the priest and to the leaders of the congregation, saying....**
**Numbers 32:2 NAS**

## Reuben and Gad: Discouragement From Settling for the Suitable

When these people saw that the land on the eastern bank of the Jordan River was suitable for livestock, what did they do? They immediately ran to the leaders of Israel.

The same thing still happens today. When there are people in our midst who are not willing to do what God has commanded or to press on to receive what He has promised, they always appeal to the leadership. Why? Because they want permission to settle for the suitable.

As leaders, we must never give people consent to settle for the suitable. Rather, we must always encourage them to press on to what God has for them. We must urge them to keep His commandments and to continue to move toward the fulfillment of His promises.

Notice what happened when these people approached Moses and the leaders of Israel: "The sons of Gad and the sons of Reuben came and *spoke* to Moses and to Eleazar the priest, and to the leaders of the congregation, *saying*...."

What did they do when they got to the leaders? They "spoke." They came "saying." They began to *speak*.

We must understand that our words have power. What we say can and does affect others as well as ourselves, just as what others say can and does have an effect upon us.

What did these people say to affect their leaders?

## Good Versus Best

"**Ataroth, Dibon, Jazer, Nimrah, Heshbon, Elealeh, Sebam, Nebo and Beon,**

**the land which the Lord conquered before the congregation of Israel, is a land for livestock; and your servants have livestock."**

**Numbers 32:3,4 NAS**

When these people came to their leaders, they used reasonings to persuade.

In the same way, when people come to us to get us to give them permission to settle for the suitable, they also come with reasonings. Sense-ruled people want to stay where things look good, and they want permission to do so.

These people came saying, "Listen, the Lord conquered this land for us, and it is good for our purposes." That was true. The Lord did conquer that land for them, and the land was good for livestock raising.

But let me point out here that just because God conquers a place for us does not mean we are supposed to stop and camp there permanently.

In our Christian pilgrimage, as we walk through this life here on earth, God is with us and for us. We are to go "from victory unto victory." God will be conquering new territory in our lives daily, weekly, monthly and yearly.

Just because God is conquering new territory and handing it over to us each day does not mean that we are to settle down and take up permanent residence there. It just means that God is working in our lives, defeating our enemies and gaining new ground for us to move through on our way to the Promised Land. We are to continue on the way until we receive the complete fulfillment of what God has promised us.

It doesn't matter what promised blessing you are endeavoring to receive from the Lord, the devil will come against you to try to hinder you from receiving it. God will be there with you, conquering in you and through you — if you continue to remain in Him. There will be smaller victories on the way to the great victory.

But just because God is conquering in your life does not mean you are supposed to stop and settle down. It just means that God is moving in your life and you must continue to move with Him "from victory unto victory."

When victories come, when new territory is gained, don't stop. Don't allow reasoning to blind you to the ultimate goal. Don't give up the best for the good. Don't fall for the temptation to settle for the suitable.

## "Don't Take Us Across the Jordan!"

**And they said, "If we have found favor in your sight, let this land be given to your servants as a possession; do not take us across the Jordan."**
**Numbers 32:5 NAS**

Because these people had experienced a small breakthrough, they wanted to settle for that minor victory instead of continuing toward the full conquest. So they began to appeal for favor or mercy from their leaders. What they really wanted was for their leaders to show pity on them and allow them to settle for this land that was suitable for their purposes, but not the land of promise suitable to God's purposes.

As men and women of God, we will be faced with the same situation. If we are not watchful, we will confuse the emotion of pity with God's mercy within us.

God's favor, mercy and grace, exhibited in wise, godly leaders, will encourage people to be faithful to Him and to continue to move toward the fulfillment of His promises to them. But if leaders are moved by pity, they will say, "Bless your heart, because you have worked so hard and waited so long with such small victory, you just go ahead and camp here on this little piece of ground that God has given you; after all, it suits you."

All the emotion of pity will do is sympathize with them, feel sorry for them, and keep them from obtaining the promise. A person can be right on the verge of obtaining the fullness of God's promise, but their leaders, moved by pity, can allow them to settle for less. It is normal for leaders to sympathize, but their feelings must not persuade them to minister less than God's promise.

It will never do anyone any good to come short of the promises of God. The only way they are going to be truly satisfied is by carrying on to complete victory.

These people begged to be given this land as a possession so they would not have to cross over the Jordan River. Now the area on the other side of the Jordan was the Promised Land. So what they were saying in essence was, "Please don't make us go into the promises of God. Let us just stay here in this place because it's suitable to us."

Here is where we must be very careful not to allow sense knowledge to appeal to the pity we feel on the inside of us. Otherwise, we will not recognize what people are actually saying to us: "Please don't make us fight the good fight of faith. Please don't make us press on to the land of promise. Just let us settle here where things are easy and comfortable."

In other words, "Don't make us live up to God's will and desire for us, but let us come short of His glory."

What is the answer to that plea?

## "You Can't Go Over by Sitting Down!"

> But Moses said to the sons of Gad and to the sons of Reuben, "Shall your brothers go to war while you yourselves sit here?"
>
> Numbers 32:6 NAS

We see here in this verse that in order to receive the fulfillment of God's promise to us, we must go to war. To enjoy all that God has for us, we must engage in a certain amount of warfare. We must go "from victory unto victory." We won't win the war if we just sit. We have got to get up and keep moving toward our final objective.

As we go, we must remember that God has promised to go with us. He will be marching by our side. He has given us the weapons we need to go forth and conquer, and He has given us His promise of victory.

### Reuben and Gad: Discouragement From Settling for the Suitable

Any time God gives a promise, He also gives provision. When we are in His will, He will make a way. He will provide the way and the means, the route and the weapons. But we must pick up those weapons and use them to fight "the good fight of faith" (1 Tim. 6:12). We must wage war, not against flesh and blood, but against principalities and powers. (Eph. 6:12.)

We need to use the name of Jesus and to remember that we have a covenant, sealed in the blood of the Lamb. We must remember that we have the Word, the Holy Scriptures, the "it is written" with which Jesus defeated Satan on the mountain of temptation. (Luke 4:1-13.)

Because Jesus defeated the enemy with the Word of God by saying again and again, "It is written," we too can succeed against the enemy by using the Word, by saying, "It is written," and then by staying in prayer.

However, we cannot wage all of our warfare in prayer. Sooner or later we must get up off our knees and onto our feet. Having put on the full armor of God (Eph. 6:11-18), we must pick up the sword of the Spirit, which is the Word, and go forth to use our God-given weapons to make progress in our own life. We have got to speak forth the name of Jesus and the Word of God. We must take action, following the directions that God gives us.

What Moses was telling the sons of Reuben and Gad was, "Listen, it is going to take warfare to conquer this land. You people can't just sit here and take it easy while the rest of your brothers go forth to win the battles for you. You have got to be a part of this campaign with us."

Yes, God is going to fight for us, but if you and I are going to reach and obtain the Promised Land (our promise), then each of us is going to have to do our part.

If you won't sit down, if you will rise up and go forth, the Lord will be there in the thick of battle with you. He will conquer for you. He will lead you through it all "from victory unto victory."

## Like Fathers, Like Sons!

> "Now why are you discouraging the sons of Israel from crossing over into the land which the Lord has given them?
> 
> "This is what your fathers did when I sent them from Kadesh-barnea to see the land."
> 
> Numbers 32:7,8 NAS

Here Moses was telling these people, "History is repeating itself. You are doing the very things that your fathers did. You are discouraging the Children of Israel from pushing on into the land promised them by the Lord. You are making their hearts melt, just as your fathers made the hearts melt in the nation of Israel forty years ago."

Moses saw that by their discouraging words, by their *sayings*, the sons of Reuben and Gad were keeping God's people from taking possession of the land the Lord had promised them.

When Moses told these people that they were doing what their fathers had done when he sent them to Kadesh-barnea to scout the land, he was referring to the spies that he had sent into Canaan forty years earlier. He was saying, "You people are being sense-ruled instead of spirit-ruled, which is the same mistake your fathers made."

You and I don't have to repeat the same mistakes that our fathers made. We can learn from them. That is what the Apostle Paul was referring to when he wrote in 1 Corinthians 10:11 NAS, "Now these things happened to them as an example, and they were written for our instruction...." That's why we study the New Testament in light of the Old Testament. We use the experiences of those who have gone before us to guide and direct us so we can avoid the mistakes they made and reap even greater blessings than they enjoyed.

## Discouragement Stops Action

"For when they went up to the valley of Eshcol and saw the land, they discouraged the sons of Israel so that they did not go into the land which the Lord had given them."

**Numbers 32:9 NAS**

Remember, in Chapter 1 we said that one of the definitions of the Hebrew words translated *discourage* in the *King James Version* was "neutralize," which we said meant to stop action.

That is exactly what happened here.

The Hebrew spies came back from their scouting trip with a negative report that totally neutralized the Children of Israel, completely stopping their action and keeping them from going in and possessing the land that had been promised to them by God.

That is a prime example of discouragement from the sayings of others.

## Following Fully

"So the Lord's anger burned in that day, and He swore, saying,

'None of the men who came up from Egypt, from twenty years old and upward, shall see the land which I swore to Abraham, to Isaac and to Jacob; for they did not follow Me fully,

except Caleb the son of Jephunneh the Kenizzite and Joshua the son of Nun, for they have followed the Lord fully.'"

**Numbers 32:10-12 NAS**

Note that although this text says that Caleb and Joshua followed the Lord *fully*, it does not say that they followed Him *perfectly*. That means that when we are trying to follow the Lord so that we can inherit all that He has promised us, we do not have to be absolutely perfect. But it does mean that those of us who receive His promised blessings are going to be those of us who have a close personal relationship with Him, those of us who put Him and His Word first and foremost in our lives.

That's the way Caleb and Joshua were. They had been part of the twelve scouts who had been sent to spy out the land of Canaan forty years earlier. They had seen the same things there that the other ten spies had seen. Yet their report was totally different from the reports of the others.

The difference between Caleb and Joshua and the other spies was that they were ruled by God while the others were ruled by their senses.

The Lord had the hearts of two of the twelve, but He did not have the hearts of the others. That's what the Lord meant when He said that, except for Caleb and Joshua, the Children of Israel did not follow Him fully. They turned away from Him in fear and doubt, so He declared that they would never see the land of promise. Their refusal to be obedient to God and to trust in Him and His Word brought eventual destruction to their lives, as it will to anyone who does not follow the Lord fully.

To refresh our memory of the story about these twelve spies, let's look back at Numbers 13.

## The Twelve Spies Are Chosen and Sent

**Then the Lord spoke to Moses saying,**

**"Send out for yourself men so that they may spy out the land of Canaan, which I am going to give to the sons of Israel; you shall send a man from each of their fathers' tribes, every one a leader among them."**

**So Moses sent them from the wilderness of Paran at the command of the Lord, all of them men who were heads of the sons of Israel.**

**Numbers 13:1-3 NAS**

Here we see that when the Children of Israel reached the edge of the Promised Land the first time, the Lord commanded Moses to choose twelve men, one from each of the twelve tribes of Israel, and to send them into the Promised Land.

In verses 4 through 15 we are given the name of each of the twelve spies, the names of their fathers and the name of each of the twelve tribes from which they were chosen.

Then beginning in verse 17 we are told what their assignment was.

## The Mission of the Spies

When Moses sent them to spy out the land of Canaan, he said to them, "Go up there into the Negev; then go up into the hill country.

"And see what the land is like, and whether the people who live in it are strong or weak, whether they are few or many.

"And how is the land in which they live, is it good or bad? And how are the cities in which they live, are they like open camps or with fortifications?

"And how is the land, is it fat or lean? Are there trees in it or not? Make an effort then to get some of the fruit of the land." Now the time was the time of the first ripe grapes.

So they went up and spied out the land from the wilderness of Zin as far as Rehob, at Lebo-hamath.

When they had gone up into the Negev, they came to Hebron where Ahiman, Sheshai and Talmai, the descendants of Anak were. (Now Hebron was built seven years before Zoan in Egypt.)

Then they came to the valley of Eshcol and from there cut down a branch with a single cluster of grapes; and they carried it on a pole between two men, with some of the pomegranates and the figs.

> That place was called the valley of Eshcol, because of the cluster which the sons of Israel cut down from there.
>
> When they returned from spying out the land, at the end of forty days,
>
> they proceeded to come to Moses and Aaron and to all the congregation of the sons of Israel in the wilderness of Paran, at Kadesh; and they brought back word to them and to all the congregation and showed them the fruit of the land.
>
> Numbers 13:17-26 NAS

After forty days, the spies who had been sent out by Moses to view the land and its people and produce returned to give their report.

Let's look at what the spies told Moses and the people about what they had seen in the land the Lord had promised to them as their new home.

## "The Land Is Good, But There Are Giants in It!"

> Thus they told him, and said, "We went in to the land where you sent us; and it certainly does flow with milk and honey, and this is its fruit.
>
> "Nevertheless, the people who live in the land are strong, and the cities are fortified and very large; and moreover, we saw the descendants of Anak there.
>
> "Amalek is living in the land of the Negev and the Hittites and the Jebusites and the Amorites are living in the hill country, and the Canaanites are living by the sea and by the side of the Jordan."
>
> Numbers 13:27-29 NAS

Remember that the descendants of Anak whom the spies met were giants.

So when the spies returned, they said, in essence, "Everything that God said about this new land is absolutely true, *but*...." Then they began to deliver what the *King James Version* calls "an evil report" (v. 32). They began to say negative things about their ability to take possession of the land that the Lord had already given to them as their inheritance.

This negative, "evil" report began to wear down the people of Israel. It caused them to become discouraged and disheartened.

Yet everything the spies were saying was just the opposite of what God through Moses had told them to do. These men had not been told to go in and determine *if* they could take the land. They had been told to go in and determine *how* they would take the land.

When they scouted out the land, they didn't see all the positives about it. All they saw were the negatives. They didn't see a land flowing with milk and honey. All they saw were the giants in the land.

Although God had told them that He had already given them the land, and they had seen how good it was, somehow when they saw the giants and the fortified cities, their faith and courage failed them and they began to doubt their ability to take possession of it.

## "We Are Grasshoppers in Our Sight and Theirs!"

Then Caleb quieted the people before Moses, and said, "We should by all means go up and take possession of it, for we shall surely overcome it."

But the men who had gone up with him said, "We are not able to go up against the people, for they are too strong for us."

So they gave out to the sons of Israel a bad report of the land which they had spied out, saying, "The land through which we have gone, in spying it out, is a land that devours its inhabitants; and all the people whom we saw in it are men of great size.

"There also we saw the Nephilim (the sons of Anak are part of the Nephilim); and we became like grasshoppers in our own sight, and so we were in their sight."

**Numbers 13:30-33 NAS**

Once they saw the giants, these people forgot what God had told them and began to measure the giants by themselves. God didn't want them to measure the giants by themselves, He wanted them to measure them by Him.

If you and I measure the giants — the devils, the problems — in our lives by ourselves, we are going to become discouraged. But if we measure them by God, we are going to be encouraged.

You and I don't have the size or the power or the ability to measure up to the giants in our lives. But God does. That's why we must measure everything by Him and His strength and ability and not by our selves and our strength and ability.

These men measured their enemies by themselves, without God, and became like grasshoppers in their own eyes and in the eyes of their enemies. They didn't go into the land to determine *how* to take it, as God had meant for them to do, but they went in to determine *if* they could take it. As a result, they came away discouraged.

You and I are not called to determine *if* we can possess the blessings that God has promised us. We are called to trust Him to show us *how* to possess them.

Caleb tried to quiet the people and assure them that with God's help they were well able to go up and defeat their enemies and take possession of the land God had given them. I believe he said over and over again, "God said...," "God said...," "God said...," reminding the people of the promises of God.

Caleb and Joshua saw the same land and the same giants the other spies saw. The difference in their report and the report of the others was that their report was based on faith, not on sight. The eyes of the others were on the power of the enemy, while the eyes of Caleb and Joshua were on the promise of the Almighty.

In this life, you are going to receive what you keep your eyes on. If your eyes are fixed and focused on a land that is suitable for cattle, then you are going to receive a land suitable for cattle. But if your eyes are fixed and focused on the promises of God, you are going to receive the fulfillment of those promises.

Never settle for *anything* less than *everything* God has promised you.

## Senses Versus Faith

In verses 11 and 12 of Numbers 32 we read that because of their lack of faith, all the nation of Israel twenty years old and older died in the wilderness. Why? Because they did not follow God fully. They did not listen to His commands and obey them. They did not keep their eyes on His promises. Instead, they allowed their hearts to become discouraged and melt because of the sayings of men.

In Numbers 13:31 these men said, "We're not able to go up against the inhabitants of this land, because they're too strong for us." In this, they were telling the absolute truth. The giants in that land were too strong for them, but the giants were not too strong for God.

When people are ruled by their senses, they forget that it is God Who will defeat their enemies. They think they have to do it themselves. That's why they fall into discouragement and defeat.

If you are going to be successful in receiving all that God has promised you in this life, then you are going to have to keep the faith. You are going to have to keep your eyes fixed and focused on the Lord and on His promise, knowing that He will fight your battles with you and for you.

Faith is nothing more than trusting God to do what He has said He will do. The Lord spoke to me and said, "So many people believe *in* Me, but do not believe *Me!*" These people didn't believe God even though they believed in Him. They listened to a bad report, and it changed the way they saw themselves. They saw themselves as grasshoppers, and so they became as grasshoppers in the eyes of their enemies.

In order to defeat you, your enemy must use discouragement to get you to take your eyes off of God and His promises. To do that, he attacks your faith. He tries to persuade and convince you that God will not do what He has promised in His Word.

If you want a real good, healthy attitude, a positive way of seeing yourself, then keep your eyes on God. He will cause you to see yourself in the right perspective, the way you need to see yourself.

These few men turned the whole nation of Israel away from God. How? By their *sayings*. They did not follow the Lord fully, and so they spoke words of discouragement before the people. Their sayings melted the hearts of the people and so, with the exception of Caleb and Joshua, an entire nation failed to press on to receive the fulfillment of God's promises.

Caleb and Joshua did receive the fulfillment of the promises. Why? Because they followed the Lord fully, not perfectly but fully. God had their hearts. And because He had their hearts, they kept their eyes on Him and His Word.

## "If You Turn Away From God, You Will Destroy People."

"So the Lord's anger burned against Israel, and He made them wander in the wilderness forty years, until the entire generation of those who had done evil in the sight of the Lord was destroyed.

"Now behold, you have risen up in your fathers' place, a brood of sinful men, to add still more to the burning anger of the Lord against Israel.

"For if you turn away from following Him, He will once more abandon them in the wilderness; and you will destroy all these people."

Numbers 32:13-15 NAS

As you remember, here in this passage Moses was speaking to the tribes of Reuben and Gad who wanted to settle for the suitable. They had asked Moses to receive their inheritance on the other side the Jordan so they wouldn't have to cross over and fight in Canaan.

Moses told them that if they turned away from following the Lord, they would destroy all the people of Israel. How would they destroy all the people? Through their sayings.

Remember, you and I can be destroyed by the sayings of others, and we can also destroy others by our sayings. What we say has an effect on people and ourselves, just as what people say has an effect on us.

If you will read on in verses 16-33 you will see that these two tribes did cross over the Jordan River and help the rest of the nation of Israel to conquer Canaan. As a reward, they received the land on the eastern bank of the Jordan for their inheritance, just as they had asked. They ended up with the suitable land because that is what they had their eyes on.

The ones who kept their eyes on the Promised Land received the fulfillment of the promises of God because they kept the faith and did what God commanded them to do. The others did not receive the full inheritance because they listened to the wrong people.

Don't allow people to dictate to you where to settle. If you do so, you will be robbed of your full inheritance. If you listen to them rather than to the Word of the Lord, you will make them the god in your life.

If you want to stay out of discouragement, don't listen to the sayings of men. And be careful of what you say to others as well as to yourself.

## Let Your Mind Dwell on These Things

**Finally, brethren, whatever is true, whatever is honorable, whatever is right, whatever is pure, whatever is lovely, whatever is of good repute, if there is any excellence and if anything worthy of praise, let your mind dwell on these things.**

**Philippians 4:8 NAS**

You and I need to minister to discouraged people. We need to help raise them up, but we must be watchful whenever we are around anyone who is negative. After we are with a negative person, we must get back into the Word of God and into prayer as soon as possible. After we have spent time with negative people, then we need to spend time with the Lord. If we don't, their negative, bad reports can overcome us and wear us down.

Keep your relationship with God pure. Keep your eyes on the good report, not the evil report. Don't allow people to stay in the negative when you're talking to them. Always interject something positive that lines up with God's Word into every conversation.

When others tear down the government, build it up. When others tear down the Church, build it up. When others tell you how bad things are in their life, remind them of the good things that are going on in their life.

Be an encourager, not a discourager.

Watch what you hear and what you say. (Mark 4:24; Matt. 12:36,37.) Don't allow your ears to be garbage pails, and don't allow your mouth to be a vehicle by which garbage is spread around.

If you will keep a guard on your ears and your mouth, you will help people rather than harm them.

According to Philippians 4:8, not only are we to guard our ears and our lips, we are also to guard our minds.

Don't allow your mind to dwell on negative, discouraging words. You should be controlling your mind, your mind should not be controlling you.

First Peter 1:13 says that we are to gird up our minds. Romans 12:2 says that we are to renew our minds. To do that, we must get into the Word of God and spend time with Him in prayer and meditation, allowing His Spirit to communicate with us and to change our old habitual patterns of thought into new ones.

Take control not only of your mind but also of your heart. In John 14:27 NAS Jesus told His disciples, "'Peace I leave with you; My peace I give to you; not as the world gives, do I give to you. Let not your heart be troubled, nor let it be fearful.'"

If we are born again, you and I have the peace of Jesus Christ, but we have to take hold of our mind, gird it up and turn it in the direction of that peace. (Is. 26:3.) How? By keeping it on God and His Word. Whenever a negative thought arises, we must take hold of it and turn it into a positive thought. We must let our mind dwell on positive things, not negative things. We do not deny the negative things, but we do deny them the power to control our thoughts.

If you want to experience the peace that passes all understanding (Phil. 4:7), then you must treat your mind like a little child. You don't allow a child to control you, to do naughty things or negative, evil things. So don't allow your mind to dwell on the naughty, evil, negative things of life. Take control of it as you would a child. You have to guide a child. You must also guide your mind and keep it on whatever is true, honorable, right, pure, lovely, of good repute, excellent and worthy of praise, even if you have to speak out loud.

Don't allow your mind to dwell on things that cause discouragement. Don't listen to negative, discouraging conversation. Watch what you hear and what you say. In some situations you may have to separate yourself from negative people. Get into the Word of God, which is sharp and powerful and can discern the thoughts and intentions of the heart. (Heb. 4:12 NAS.) Turn from the evil and dwell on the good. Remember and believe what God says, not what people say!

## Six Keys to Handling Discouragement

To wrap up this chapter, let's review the six key ways we have discussed of handling discouragement:

1. Turn your discouragement over to God. Let Him take the burdens and pressures of responsibility off of you.

2. Don't settle for the suitable. Don't camp until you have received the fulfillment of the promise.

3. Don't judge by what your eyes see, but use righteous judgment. Don't listen to negative, discouraging reports, but instead listen to the Holy Spirit.

4. Follow God fully, which may not always be perfectly. When you do make a mistake, learn from it and go on. Keep your eyes fixed and focused on God and His Word.

5. Don't let anything or anyone turn you from following the path that God has laid out for you.

6. Don't give heed to negative people and don't be a negative person yourself. Remember that sayings can bring destruction. Watch what you hear and what you say. Keep your mind and heart and mouth on those things that are true, honorable, right, pure, lovely, of good repute, excellent

and worthy of praise. Don't be overcome by evil — by discouraging words — but always overcome evil with good. (Rom. 12:21.)

# 5
# Israel: Discouragement From Troubles Along the Way

And they [the Children of Israel] journeyed from mount Hor by the way of the Red sea, to compass the land of Edom: and the soul of the people was much discouraged because of the way.

Numbers 21:4

The *New American Standard Bible* translates this phrase "discouraged by the way" as "impatient because of the journey."

Sometimes in our Christian walk we do become discouraged by the way, impatient because of the journey. We want to get where we are going. We don't like detours, setbacks or side trips. That was the problem with the Israelites.

## "You Shall Not Pass Through!"

From Kadesh Moses then sent messengers to the king of Edom: "Thus your brother Israel has said, 'You know all the hardship that has befallen us;

that our fathers went down to Egypt, and we stayed in Egypt a long time, and the Egyptians treated us and our fathers badly.

'But when we cried out to the Lord, He heard our voice and sent an angel and brought us out from Egypt; now behold, we are at Kadesh, a town on the edge of your territory.

'Please let us pass through your land. We shall not pass through field or through vineyard; we shall not even drink water from a well. We shall go along the king's highway, not turning to the right or left, until we pass through your territory.'"

Edom, however, said to him, "You shall not pass through us, lest I come out with the sword against you."

Again, the sons of Israel said to him, "We shall go up by the highway, and if I and my livestock do drink any of your water, then I will pay its price. Let me only pass through on my feet, nothing else."

But he said, "You shall not pass through." And Edom came out against him with a heavy force, and with a strong hand.

Thus Edom refused to allow Israel to pass through his territory; so Israel turned away from him.

**Numbers 20:14-21 NAS**

In this passage we see that the direct route from Egypt to Canaan was closed to the Israelites because of the refusal of the king of Edom to allow them to cross through his territory. As a result, they were compelled to move southward, then eastward, and then northward toward Moab. They spent a number of days going through the Arabah, which was "a mountain plain of loose sand, gravel and rock...."[1]

It was here that we are told that the Israelites became "impatient because of the journey."

## Detour to Discouragement

And the people spoke against God and Moses, "Why have you brought us up out of Egypt to die in the wilderness? For there is no food and no water, and *we loathe this miserable food.*"

**Numbers 21:5 NAS**

---

[1] Finis Jennings Dake, *Dake's Annotated Reference Bible* (Lawrenceville, GA: Dake Bible Sales, 1963), p. 180.

## Israel: Discouragement From Troubles Along the Way

This "miserable food" the people were referring to was *the manna provided for them by God*. Since there was no water to drink, and *only manna* to eat, when the people became "much discouraged" they began to complain about the manna they were eating as though it were not enough.

They were impatient because of the journey, discouraged by the way they were required to travel to the land of promise. They had set out on a direct course, but had been forced to detour. They wanted to take a straight route, but it was blocked, so they had to sidetrack through a barren and inhospitable land. As a result, they became discouraged and started complaining about manna as well as the lack of water.

Now I must break to you a bit of bad news. As you and I make our journey through life, as we walk with the Lord "on the way," there will be times when we will meet Edomites who want to refuse us direct passage through their territory to our destination. Their purpose is to force us to go aside, become discouraged, give up the journey and to desire "other food" rather than what God provides. If we give up the true manna (God's Word), we will allow the detour to stop us!

The Children of Israel were getting close to the fulfillment of their promise and had to detour because of the enemy. They began to grumble about the manna and wanted to enjoy natural foods. The hope of enjoyment that seemed so near, when thwarted, brought disappointment, which led to a depression of spirits. In this state they began to speak against God's provision — the manna of "light" bread.

They called it "light" bread because of its lack of substance, considering it fit only for children. They were eating the food of angels, which they considered contemptible, even though it had kept them for forty years. They had their eyes on the enjoyment of what was to come, rather than on the One Who had made the provision.

Whether you and I are in the midst of the wilderness or the promise, God is still the Provider, and we must keep our eyes on Him at all times. These people put their eyes on their circumstances and the enemy, thus allowing their fleshly desire for a better life to overwhelm their trust and faith in God's ability to nourish them, keep them strong and bring them into the fulfillment of the promise.

If you and I keep our eyes only on the journey and the enjoyment of what is to come, and not on God the Provider, when something happens to delay the fulfillment of the promise we will become "much discouraged." We will allow a depression of our spirit to take us beyond discouragement and into depression.

Delays happen and roads are sometimes detoured, but God is still our Provider. He still knows where we are and has a way to make a crooked path straight. So we must keep our eyes on Him.

Just because "Edom" steps in and closes the door to the route that would take us directly to our goal, we must not do as the Israelites did. We must not become discouraged and complain because of a lack of natural food and water. We must turn to the food that God provides, which will more than keep us on this journey through life.

## The Dangers of "Low-Word Pressure"

The food we need is the Word of God. Without it, our mental and emotional immune system breaks down. We become weakened and vulnerable to discouragement.

That's why I am encouraging you that as you continue your daily walk with the Lord, be sure to partake daily of the manna that He has provided for you. In such trying times, it is imperative to keep ingesting "the bread of life."

Some believers read their Bible and think, "I'm not getting anything out of this," so they quit. But it is as vital to keep spiritual food going into the spirit as it is to keep natural food going into the body.

As human beings, our spirit thrives, grows and becomes strong as we partake of the Word of God. Our minds are programmed and our hearts are strengthened by feeding on the Word.

The Bible says that faith comes by hearing, and hearing by the Word of God. (Rom. 10:17.) If you are being attacked by discouragement, if your faith is weak and anemic, then you may be suffering from spiritual malnutrition. You may need to check your "food intake" to make sure that your "Word level" is not low.

## The Water of the Spirit

These people also suffered because of a lack of water. I believe the water image here is a reference to the need of being continually filled with the Holy Spirit.

In 1 Corinthians 10:1-4 NAS the Apostle Paul wrote of these people: "For I do not want you to be unaware, brethren, that our fathers were all under the cloud, and all passed through the sea; and all were baptized into Moses in the cloud and in the sea; and all ate the same spiritual food; and all drank the same spiritual drink, for they were drinking from a spiritual rock which followed them; and the rock was Christ."

Later in 1 Corinthians 12:13 NAS Paul wrote: "For by one Spirit we were all baptized into one body, whether Jews or Greeks, whether slaves or free, and we were all made to drink of one Spirit."

If you and I are to remain spiritually strong and healthy like our spiritual forefathers, we must continue to eat of the Word and drink of the Holy Spirit.

Without food we will become undernourished and starve to death, and without water we will become dehydrated and die. To be healthy we need both.

It is the Word of God, the manna, the bread of heaven, that *imparts* knowledge to us. It is the Holy Spirit, the water of life, that *reveals* knowledge to us. Without the Spirit, the Word is dead. Without the Word, the Spirit has nothing to water.

We must have the Word of God planted in our hearts, and we must have the Spirit of God to water that Word and cause it to bring forth fruit. It takes both of these to keep our spirits alive and growing. Then we will be strong and healthy, able to stand against impatience and keep discouragement at bay.

As you make your way, your journey, through the wilderness of life, I encourage you to continually eat of the Word and drink of the Spirit in order to remain in the joy of the Lord — which is the source of your strength. (Neh. 8:10.)

## A Way That Won't Work

Just as these people followed a way that did not work, so we will find ourselves having to face ways that will not work for us. Just as they had to take a detour and ended up facing a desert plain that seemed to offer no hope, so we will find ourselves at times in difficult and discouraging circumstances.

Does that mean we should give up and quit? Does it mean we are never going to reach our goal? Does it mean we have somehow gotten out of the will of God?

No! It just means we have found a way that will not work. Therefore, instead of complaining and becoming totally discouraged and defeated, we have to go to God and ask Him to show us a way that will work.

Whatever happens to you in your daily walk with the Lord, never give up and never quit. Keep right on going and sooner or later He will show you the way.

## The Irritation of Sand

As I reflected on the three types of elements that made up the plain of Arabah where the Children of Israel found themselves, I decided to do some research into the subject. From the dictionary, the concordance and several Bible commentaries, I learned some things about each of these natural features which I believe have a spiritual correlation. Let's look at each of them separately, beginning with sand.

As we know, sand is irritating. If you have ever walked on a beach and gotten sand in your shoes or sandals, you know how it can cause *irritation*, which Webster defines as "an excessive response to stimulation" or "a sore or inflamed condition."[2]

Thus, sand represents all the little minor things that we encounter in our daily lives. If we do not keep ourselves full of the Word and Spirit of God, they will cause us problems. They will become irritating to us and cause us to respond excessively to them. They will produce a sore or inflamed condition in our spirit that will cause us to become impatient and discouraged.

The Word and Spirit of God help to keep our everyday lives in proper balance. They keep the love of God stirred up on the inside of us.

In Jude 20 the Bible tells us to pray in the Holy Spirit, keeping ourselves in the love of God. When we are operating in the love of God, all of the other fruit of His Spirit will follow. (Gal. 5:22,23.) When that happens, we are not as easily irritated by everything that goes wrong in our life. We find ourselves not responding excessively to the stimulation of the many minor problems that beset us as we live from day to day.

---

[2] Webster, s.v. "irritation."

Without the Word of God planted in our spirit and the Spirit of God to water it, we will be much more likely to become irritated by minor problems. We will be much more likely to become critical and judgmental. Like the Children of Israel, if we allow things or other people to continue to irritate us, we may eventually become discouraged and even angry and rebellious.

However, if we will allow the Word to take root in our hearts and minds, and if we will continue to water it with the Spirit, it will grow and produce the fruit of the Spirit within us. Then, as we act on the Word, we will be stimulated to respond in a godly manner, no matter how irritating the outward stimulation or situation may be.

## The Discomfort of Gravel

The next thing these people ran into was gravel.

That is what often happens. If the sand, the minor irritation, is not taken care of, it will grow into larger problems.

Since gravel is made up of bigger elements than sand, it is less of an irritation and more of a discomfort. The dictionary defines the word *discomfort* as a "lack of comfort," "inconvenience," or "distress."[3]

If minor irritations are left unchecked, they will grow in magnitude and will end up causing not only a lack of comfort and an inconvenience but actual distress.

These are the kinds of things that produce a lack of control. I say that because we all know that when we get sand in our shoe or sandal, it causes a minor irritation, but when we get a piece of gravel in our shoe or sandal it causes real discomfort. If the cause of that discomfort is not

---

[3]*Webster's New World Dictionary, Concise Edition*, s.v. "discomfort."

removed quickly, it will soon become the focal point of our attention. Our entire mind will be focused on that problem. It will begin to consume our thoughts, and when that happens we will have lost control of our own mental processes.

If you and I don't handle well the minor irritations in our lives, we may allow the enemy to set us up for more serious problems. Minor irritations may grow into more important discomforts.

If other people discover that we can be easily irritated and annoyed, they may either try to avoid us altogether or to aggravate us on purpose in order to cause us grief and misery.

The enemy will certainly do everything in his power to cause us problems so that we lose the respect and approval of others. Unless we learn to control our reactions to minor irritations and more serious discomforts, we may wind up losing our personal reputation as well as our Christian influence.

We in the Church of Jesus Christ must understand and realize that we have a responsibility to live the Christian life before those around us. We bring on ourselves many of the irritations and inconveniences we deal with day to day, because we are not full of the Word and Spirit of God; therefore we do not manifest the fruit of His Spirit.

We need to stay full of the Word and Spirit of God because it is then that we are able to walk securely. The righteous are to walk securely in this life with the angels of God encamped around about us. But if we are not in close relationship and fellowship with God through His Word and Spirit, there will be repercussions in our daily lives. Things will go wrong; there will be all kinds of irritations, inconveniences and discomforts to cause us to lose our peace, our joy, our strength and our witness for the Lord.

We must remember that there is a devil out there who wants to bring problems to the Church and to the individual members of it. He does that to try to keep us from fulfilling the call of God on our lives, from doing the work of the Lord and from reaching the goal that our heavenly Father has set before us.

Just because you and I are full of the Word and Spirit of God does not mean that our enemy is not going to try to bring irritations, inconveniences and discomforts into our lives to get us to lose control. But it does mean that we can learn how to handle these things. Even if the enemy does bring these things upon us, and he will, we are able to handle them because greater is He Who is in us than he who is in the world (1 John 4:4) and because we can do all things through Christ Who strengthens us. (Phil. 4:13.)

The irritations, the inconveniences and the discomforts are still out there. Jesus has told us that in this life we will have tribulations. God has never promised us that we will not encounter tribulations. But the Lord has said that He will *keep us* in this world. He has said that He has overcome the world and that through Him we are overcomers too.

There is sand and gravel in our world, just as there was sand and gravel in the world in which the Children of Israel found themselves. But we don't have to make the same mistake they made and fall into discouragement by griping and complaining. We can keep our eyes on the goal, confident that we are going to make it despite the obstacles that the enemy throws in our path, despite the detours that we may have to take, and despite all the irritations and discomforts we may encounter along the way.

How? By doing what the Children of Israel did not do! They loathed the manna from heaven and complained because they did not have natural food and water. Let's appreciate God's food and water and not try to replace it with the food and water of the world.

Then we will be triumphant!

The knowledge and assurance of the Word will carry us through to victory in Jesus!

## The Rocks of Trouble

Because they grumbled and griped through the sand, and murmured and complained through the gravel, the Children of Israel ended up on the rocks — which are larger than the gravel or the sand. The size of their problems steadily increased in magnitude.

That's the way the devil works. Give him a toehold and he will put in his knee and then his thigh and then his whole body. The way to defeat him is to stop him when he first tries to stick in his big toe. You do this, as we have said before, by submitting to God and His Word, resisting the devil in that submission — and then the devil will flee. If you don't, then he will worm his way in bit by bit.

That's what happened to these people. They went from the sand of irritation to the gravel of discomfort to the rocks of trouble.

One of the dictionary definitions of the word *rocks* is "something that threatens or causes disaster," as in the phrase "their marriage went on the rocks," meaning "in or into a state of destruction or wreckage."[2] In other words, in this context the word rocks means trouble.

In the verb form, the word *trouble* means to "agitate," "worry," or "harass."[3] As a noun, it means "annoyance," "suffering," "a difficult or unhappy situation" or "disturbance."[4]

---

[2] *Webster's Ninth New Collegiate Dictionary*, s.v. "rock."

[3] *Webster's New World Dictionary, Concise Edition*, s.v. "trouble."

[4] *Webster's New World Dictionary, Young People's Edition*, s.v. "trouble."

As you know, being agitated is a greater problem than being irritated. You and I can have little irritations in this life and still function without other people being aware of what is going on inside of us. We can be in discomfort, or uncomfortable, without others being aware of it. But when we are agitated, people usually know it.

Agitation generally shows on the countenance. It may even be noticed in the movements of the body. There may be twitches or an inability to sit still.

When I think of the word agitate, I usually picture a washing machine with the agitator constantly in motion. Often that is the way people act when they become troubled or agitated. Instead of sitting down quietly and patiently reading the Bible or praying in the Spirit until they calm down and hear from the Lord, they try to handle things in their own way — and usually end up making matters worse.

When people are agitated, they often worry about everything around them. Such people allow the things of life to have such an effect on them that they become distrustful even of those who want to help them.

That is exactly what happened to the Children of Israel. Because they found themselves in a desert place without any food or water, they allowed themselves to become discouraged, irritated, discomforted and even troubled. In that state they became distrustful of those around them, especially of their leaders, those who were doing the most to help them.

## The Rocks of Harassment

As we have seen, one of the definitions of the verb form of the word *trouble* is "harass." The devil loves to harass God's people.

In John 10:10, Jesus said that Satan comes only to steal, kill and destroy. The devil knows that in order to kill and destroy God's children, he first has to steal the Word of God from them.

If Satan can manage to steal from you and me the Word of God and our fellowship with the Father through the Holy Spirit, then he can bring upon us all kinds of harassment — mental, physical, emotional and spiritual. He will harass us constantly until we can no longer function properly. When that happens, we are in trouble.

But even if you are in that condition right now, I want to encourage you that it is not too late. Turn to God. He is right there with you, and He will help you.

Even if you are being harassed by the enemy, even if you are in trouble, even if you are agitated and distrustful, you can still turn to God and He will deliver you from all your troubles. (Ps. 34:17.)

Have you ever found yourself in a situation in which it seemed that everywhere you turned you were having problems? You were looking for your income tax refund to arrive so you could pay off those overdue bills, and day after day it just didn't come. At the same time you had ordered cassette tapes from the world's greatest evangelist's latest campmeeting, and they never arrived. Then, one of your co-workers turned against you for no reason and began to say things about you that weren't true. Next, you experienced a troublesome situation in your family life — a death or sickness or divorce or argument that split the family wide open so that loved ones weren't speaking to each other. Finally, to top it all off, you went to church on Sunday morning to seek some relief and comfort, and everyone there seemed to be avoiding you — and you didn't know why any of this was happening to you.

Have you ever been through that kind of ordeal? If you have, you probably thought to yourself, "It seems like I'm just being *harassed*!" Well, you were! You were being harassed by the enemy.

The reason you and I come under harassment most of the time is simply because we have an enemy who hates and despises us because we belong to God and worship and serve Him. However, sometimes we allow that kind of harassment to happen to us because we have moved out of the will and way of the Lord. In that case, we need to make an adjustment and turn back to God. We must go back to the place we last heard Him and obey what He has said without grumbling and complaining. Then He will deliver us.

If you find yourself in that kind of troubling situation, turn back to the Lord. You may still have to go out of your way, but if you will turn to the Lord and ask for His wisdom, guidance and strength, He will be there with you to help you. Just remember that as long as you are *in* Christ, you are *in* the way.

If we are willing to listen to Him, God can take even our failures and mistakes, our waywardness and wrong decisions, and turn them for good for us and for others. In our willingness we will become obedient. In our obedience we will begin to eliminate those mistakes and failures of the past, because obedience to God means being on the right path physically, mentally and spiritually. *His* path *is* the way of victory, no matter how it looks.

## The Rocks of Difficulty and Disturbance

Another definition of the noun form of the word *trouble* is "a difficult or unhappy situation" or "disturbance."

In this world, there are many difficulties and disturbances. Just like everyone else, you and I are going to have to face them and deal with them. The way we deal with them has to do with our relationship with the Father, the Son and the Holy Spirit.

In these pages I am not telling you that because you are a believer you will never be discouraged. I am simply telling you that you do not have to give in to and be held down by discouragement. Because you are in Christ, your attitude can be so positive and your purpose so determined that you simply will not allow discouragement to take control of you. If you are not full of God and His Word and Spirit, the way you perceive things can allow discouragement to drag you down into depression.

Don't let discouragement get a hold on you and drag you down; instead, overcome discouragement by laying hold of hope. What hope? The hope that is ours in Christ, "which hope we have as an *anchor* of the soul, both sure and stedfast..." (Heb. 6:19).

In John 16:33 Jesus told His disciples, "These things have I spoken unto you, that in me ye might have peace. In the world ye shall have tribulation [harassment, difficulty, disturbance]: but be of good cheer; I have overcome the world."

Do you want to be in the world or in Christ? In the world there are troubles, difficulties, disturbances, harassments and agitations, but if you are in Christ then you can overcome all these things just as He overcame the world.

There are many things happening every day around the world and even in our own neighborhoods and churches and families that are troubling and disturbing. But what Jesus was telling us is, how we handle the problems in the world *around* us will depend on how much of the Word and Spirit of God we have *within* us.

## Full of the Word and Spirit or Yielded to the Word and Spirit?

Although it is vitally important to be filled with the Word and Spirit of God, in order to overcome the enemy and his attacks against us we must do more than that — we must be continuously yielded to the Word and Spirit that we have within us.

To yield to God's Word and His Holy Spirit is to yield to God Himself.

In Hebrews 4:12 AMP we are told that the Word of God is "...alive and full of power [making it active, operative, energizing, and effective]; it is sharper than any two-edged sword, penetrating to the dividing line of the breath of life (soul) and [the immortal] spirit, and of joints and marrow [of the deepest parts of our nature], exposing and sifting and analyzing and judging the very thoughts and purposes of the heart."

That means that when we take in the Word of God, it goes down into the joints and marrow and begins to have an effect on our thoughts and the intents of our heart. It goes into our innermost being to do a work and bring about a change in us and in our attitude and outlook. It changes our whole perception of life.

Part of that change in perception concerns the way we view the "tribulations" of life. Instead of seeing them as sand (irritations), or gravel (discomforts) or rocks (troubles), we begin to see them as opportunities to display God's power in us. We begin to realize that we have the power within us to walk through them, around them or over them. They are still there, but they don't change us, we change them.

That's the difference between being *full* of the Word and the Spirit and being *yielded* to the Word and the Spirit.

## Keep Your Eyes on the Prize

The mistake the Children of Israel made was focusing on the wrong things. Instead of keeping their eyes on God and their destination, the Promised Land over the horizon, they kept them on the difficulty, the sand and gravel and rocks beneath their feet. They let the irritations, discomforts and troubles of the present keep them from seeing the vision of the future given to them by God.

Sure, they had to detour a bit. They had to go north and south and east and west of what *they* thought was the correct way. But God knew all the time that if they would keep their eyes on Him, they would reach their goal, because He was the goal, the destination, their "exceeding great reward" (Gen. 15:1).

If the Children of Israel had kept their eyes on the Lord, He would have kept their vision ever shining before them. But because they kept their eyes on the sand, the gravel and the rocks, they became discouraged.

What are your eyes focused on? Are they on your difficulties or are they on your destination? Are they on the problems or the promise? Do you have a goal? Have you sought God? Have you built a relationship with Him and received from Him the vision that you are to follow after in this life?

You cannot ignore the problems that surround you daily, but when you have your eyes on God instead of your problems, you can handle them. You and God together can overcome all the obstacles that the enemy throws in your path to keep you from reaching the goal, fulfilling the vision and enjoying the abundant life that God has for you.

If something is happening in your life to cause you to become discouraged, don't allow that discouragement to take such a hold on you that it drags you down into depression and despondency. Instead, grab hold of God and allow Him to lift you up to peace and joy.

Don't keep your eyes on the irritations, discomforts and troubles that surround you. You cannot ignore them, but don't dwell on them, don't give them your undivided attention. Instead, fix and focus your sight on God and He will show you the way to walk through, around or over the obstacles in your path.

Again, I am not saying you should ignore your problems, but you should keep them in the proper perspective. See them through the eyes of God and allow Him to reveal to you how to solve them.

The difference in how you perceive and handle the problems of life depends on whether or not you have a relationship with God through His Word and His Spirit and are embracing them and yielding to them, or whether you are being fooled into thinking that you can do without your spiritual food and water.

If you are in discouragement right now, I encourage you to run as quickly as you can to the Word and the Spirit. Yield to them and allow them to bring about the change that is needed in you. Allow the power of God to rise up on the inside of you to take care of those problems.

## Take Jesus as Your Example

Your way or journey may be a little rough right now. But you must keep asking yourself, "Where am I going?"

Are you just wandering around here and there and everywhere or do you have a destination and a goal? Are you eating and drinking properly to give you the nourishment you need to strengthen and sustain you for the journey across the sand, the gravel and the rocks to reach that destination and attain that goal?

A lack of food and water makes the sand, gravel and rocks harder to bear.

Isaiah prophesied that the coming Messiah would not fail or become discouraged until He had finished His course. (Is. 42:4.) Even though Jesus had to face the same kinds of problems that you and I face in this life, He never allowed discouragement to keep Him from fulfilling His God-given mission.

If you have received Jesus as Savior and Lord, then you need to remember that the same Spirit that dwelled in Him also dwells in you — and He is there for the same purpose He was in Jesus.

If you haven't received Jesus as your Savior and Lord, you can remedy that situation right now. You can ask Him to come into your heart and be the Savior, Lord and Master of your life. You can acknowledge that He died in your place, that He went to the cross, that He was crucified, that He died and was buried and that He rose again from the dead and now sits on the right hand of God the Father. Because He did all that for you, because He died, rose again and lives forever, you can live. Because He paid the price, you can reap the benefit.

If you have done that, then you are born again or born of the Spirit. (John 3:5-8.) Now you need to remember the Spirit of Whom you have been born. He dwells in you just as He dwelled in Jesus. He is there to strengthen, guide, direct and empower you, just as He did for Jesus in His days on this earth.

And just as Jesus was faithful to His God-given mission, just as He did not quit until He had fulfilled the will of God for His life, so you must do the same.

The reason Jesus did not become discouraged and quit, I believe, was because of His close relationship and fellowship with the Father. I also believe that it was because of that close relationship and fellowship that He knew He could do whatever God asked Him to do.

Don't you think that in the Garden of Gethsemane Jesus was discouraged? But in that discouragement, to Whom did He turn? He turned to God the Father. He prayed that if possible the cup of suffering might pass from Him. But then

He added, "But Your will be done, Father, not Mine." (Luke 22:42.) He clung to the Father, knowing that in His close relationship and fellowship with God He could endure whatever lay ahead of Him.

The Bible says that Jesus was "...obedient unto death, even the death of the cross" (Phil. 2:8). Yet through it all He did not get discouraged, but looked to God, Who "...was able to save him..." (Heb. 5:7). For our sake, He "...endured the cross, despising the shame, and is set down at the right hand of the throne of God" (Heb. 12:2).

Jesus had to go through some hard times, but through them all He kept His eyes on His destination and His goal. He depended on God to take Him through to victory. He did not quit or sit down until He had completed His God-ordained course and said, "It is finished." (John 19:30.)

Like Jesus, you cannot sit down, you cannot quit, until you have finished your course. Get up! Get in the Word, get in the Spirit, and begin again. Allow God to give you the strength and courage you need to go through and do what He wants you to do. Get your eyes fixed and focused on your destination. Keep looking to God and not at your surroundings. Let Him put your surroundings in the proper perspective.

## Resist the Temptation to Become Discouraged

Don't allow the devil to distort what is going on around you. If you let him, the enemy will amplify and magnify the problems that beset you on all sides. Like sand and gravel and rocks, if he can get in he will irritate, discomfort and trouble you, causing you to lose control. He will agitate and harass you and cause you to take your eyes from the Word and focus them on the world. When you do that, he will rob you of the vital spiritual food and water you must have to keep going. He will weaken you so he can kill and destroy you.

Discouragement is a deadly weapon of the enemy. But I want you to know that the Lord has triumphed over Satan and his weapons. The Bible says that Jesus Christ defeated Satan at the cross of Calvary. (Col. 2:14,15.) His victory was your victory. Now you just need to learn to walk in that victory.

The Bible also says that Jesus was tempted in every way "like as we are" (Heb. 4:15). I don't know about you, but it helps me to realize that Jesus went through exactly what you and I are going through right now. And He did not stop. He did not quit until He had finished His course. He did not give into discouragement. Instead, He relied on and trusted Himself to the Spirit of God. And because you and I are in Him, we have the same Spirit on the inside of us.

If you will walk in fellowship with God through Jesus Christ, if you will partake of and yield to the Word and the Spirit, you will be strengthened and empowered to go through to victory.

Now, as we have said, you may have discovered a way that will not work. But that is no disgrace. That has happened to most of us at one time or another and will probably happen again. Disgrace is not falling down, it is staying down, it is refusing to use the strength and power at our disposal to get back up and overcome the enemy and his devises (2 Cor. 2:11) — one of which is discouragement.

It is my heart's desire to encourage and inspire you and all others who have come under discouragement to get up and go again. Slam the door in the devil's face. When you do so, it will be God's power that is behind that closed door. Yield to God and He will give you the power to resist the devil and overcome him so that he flees from you. (James 4:7.)

Discouragement is a heavy burden. It is like a weight around the neck. If you don't cut the cord that holds it in place, it will eventually choke you. Cast off that burden and fix your eyes on the goal. Keep moving forward and don't stop until you have fulfilled your vision. Don't quit until you have received every blessing, the full inheritance, that God has laid up for you.

What has God asked you to do? What is His vision for you? What course has He laid out for you to follow? Do what He has asked, seek to fulfill the vision He has given you, follow that course He has laid out for you without wavering or faltering. You can do what God has called you to do. You can make it all the way, you can complete the journey, you can finish the course, even if you have to make a detour to do so. You can do it through Jesus Christ Who strengthens you. (Phil. 4:13.)

You may not reach it overnight, but you will get there. You may have to put up with some sand, gravel and rocks along the way, but you will make it. If you do not grow weary in well doing, you will reap the reward of your effort — if you faint not. (Gal. 6:9.)

You didn't get to the place you are now without effort, and you won't get to the place God has called you to be without effort. But with His help and guidance, sooner or later you will get there.

I encourage you to rise up and take your rightful place in the Body of Christ.

# 6
# David: Discouragement From Rebellion

My heart's cry is for you to come out of discouragement and depression — or to avoid them if you are not trapped in them now.

Allow me to share one more incident in the Bible in which a man had a great opportunity to be in the depths of discouragement, depression and despair, and what he did to overcome it.

David's own son Absalom rose up against him. There had been family problems of incest, murder and banishment (2 Sam. 13-14) and from these events I believe bitterness and revenge arose in Absalom's heart. As a result, he plotted against his father to take his kingdom.

Rebellion in the heart of Absalom led him as he put his plan into action. If bitterness and revenge are allowed to remain in the heart, they will fester until there is a movement toward rebellion. That is what Absalom did. He harbored bitterness and revenge in his heart, and the resulting rebellion led him to attempt to overthrow his father, David, and take his place as king.

One of the characteristics of rebellion is the desire to build up self while tearing down another. This kind of attitude is born out of defiance against authority or outside control.

Rebellion stems from an attitude that says, "*I* am not getting a fair shake. *I* could do much better than my superiors. How dare they act without consulting *me*? How dare they do this to *me*?"

This kind of response is evidence to me that this person has a hard time submitting to those in authority over him. If he cannot or will not abide by their decisions, but instead allows this kind of self-centered attitude to remain, it will ultimately lead to the destruction of himself and of others.

Absalom allowed this kind of attitude to remain and proceeded to do everything he could to turn the people of Israel against David. At the same time, he was building himself up in their eyes. As an enemy, he was both patient and deceptive.

Rebellion is devious and cunning and will wait until its plan is ready to spring. Absalom worked his plan for years right under David's nose, until he felt the time was right. He then began to send spies to the people who had served David the king and in whom he had planted seeds of doubt and frustration. (2 Sam. 15:10,11.)

Let's look at the story from the beginning to see what happened and how David reacted to it.

## Absalom Steals the Hearts of Israel

And it came to pass after this, that Absalom prepared him chariots and horses, and fifty men to run before him.

And Absalom rose up early, and stood beside the way of the gate: and it was so, that when any man that had a controversy came to the king for judgment, then Absalom called unto him, and said, Of what city art thou? And he said, Thy servant is of one of the tribes of Israel.

And Absalom said unto him, See, thy matters are good and right; but there is no man deputed of the king to hear thee.

> Absalom said moreover, Oh that I were made judge in the land, that every man which hath any suit or cause might come unto me, and I would do him justice!
>
> And it was so, that when any man came nigh to him to do him obeisance, he put forth his hand, and took him, and kissed him.
>
> And on this manner did Absalom to all Israel that came to the king for judgment: so Absalom stole the hearts of the men of Israel.
>
> 12 Samuel 15:1-6

Absalom stole the hearts of the people of Israel by insinuating that the king was too busy for them, but that *he*, Absalom, would always be available to them. He was guilty of literally "kissing up" to them to win their hearts.

Rebellion plants seeds of doubt, frustration and insinuation as it patiently waits to attack.

## Rebellious People Draw Rebels

> And with Absalom went two hundred men out of Jerusalem, that were called; and they went in their simplicity, and they knew not any thing.
>
> And Absalom sent for Ahithophel the Gilonite, David's counseller, from his city, even from Giloh, while he offered sacrifices. And the conspiracy was strong; for the people increased continually with Absalom.
>
> 2 Samuel 15:11,12

Rebellious people gather rebellious people around them.

Absalom worked within David's own people and house to overthrow him. He sought out those who wanted revenge against David. He sent for Ahithophel, David's counselor, whom he knew as Bathsheba's grandfather. It is supposed that Ahithophel wanted to avenge the family name for what David had done to Bathsheba and to them.

Not only was Absalom someone very close to David, someone David trusted, but he was also someone who pretended to serve the Lord as David did.

Because we love them, often we do not detect those close to us who are operating in false piety. Blinded by our love, we give them our trust and blessing, as David did with his son Absalom.

## The Wilderness of Discouragement

> And there came a messenger to David, saying, The hearts of the men of Israel are after Absalom.
>
> And David said unto all his servants that were with him at Jerusalem, Arise, and let us flee; for we shall not else escape from Absalom: make speed to depart, lest he overtake us suddenly, and bring evil upon us, and smite the city with the edge of the sword.
>
> And the king's servants said unto the king, Behold, thy servants are ready to do whatsoever my lord the king shall appoint.
>
> And the king went forth, and all his household after him. And the king left ten women, which were concubines, to keep the house.
>
> And the king went forth, and all the people after him, and tarried in a place that was far off....
>
> And all the country wept with a loud voice, and all the people passed over: the king also himself passed over the brook Kidron, and all the people passed over, toward the way of the wilderness.
>
> 2 Samuel 15:13-17,23

David finally heard of Absalom's plot and of the rebellion of those who followed him. David and all who were with him had to run for their lives and found themselves in the wilderness.

What a discouraging day for David to learn of this rebellion in his midst by someone he loved and held dear to him. What a wilderness to be in — the wilderness of discouragement.

## David's Uncertainty and Trust

> And lo Zadok also, and all the Levites were with him, bearing the ark of the covenant of God: and they set down the ark of God; and Abiathar went up, until all the people had done passing out of the city.
> 
> And the king said unto Zadok, Carry back the ark of God into the city: if I shall find favour in the eyes of the Lord, he will bring me again, and shew me both it, and his habitation:
> 
> But if he thus say, I have no delight in thee; behold, here am I, let him do to me as seemeth good unto him.
> 
> The king said also unto Zadok the priest, Art thou not a seer? return into the city in peace, and your two sons with you, Ahimaaz thy son, and Jonathan the son of Abiathar.
> 
> See, I will tarry in the plain of the wilderness, until there come word from you to certify me.
> 
> 2 Samuel 15:24-28

In this wilderness experience David became uncertain: "Is God doing this to me, or is it strictly Absalom's doing?" He determined to put his trust in God to bring him back home to his kingdom again while he waited in the wilderness for a good word.

You may have found that rebellion dwells in your midst and is attacking you. You too may be uncertain as to its origin. But let me encourage you to do as David did. Trust in God to bring you back again. While you are wondering what to do, wait for a good word from the Lord.

Only God has the answer you need.

## David Weeps

> Zadok therefore and Abiathar carried the ark of God again to Jerusalem: and they tarried there.

> And David went up by the ascent of mount Olivet, and wept as he went up, and had his head covered, and he went barefoot: and all the people that was with him covered every man his head, and they went up, weeping as they went up.
>
> 2 Samuel 15:29,30

Here we see David climbing up the Mount of Olives, weeping as he went, with his head covered and his feet bare.

In those days, covering the head and walking barefoot were symbols of mourning.

This was not an easy time for David. He was running for his life and being chased by his own son, one who was close to him in every way.

Where David had been wearing a crown and sitting on a throne, now he had his head covered in mourning and was walking up a hill with his feet bare. Where he had been filled with joy, now he was weeping in sorrow and discouragement.

This discouragement affected not only David, but all those who were with him. They too covered their heads and wept bitterly as they climbed the hill of the Lord.

## David Prays

> And one told David, saying, Ahithophel is among the conspirators with Absalom. And David said, O Lord, I pray thee, turn the counsel of Ahithophel into foolishness.
>
> 2 Samuel 15:31

It was bad enough to lose his throne and his son and have to run for his life, but now David learns that his own counselor Ahithophel is one of the conspirators with Absalom.

This was a man who was respected by the people and who had been mightily used of God to speak His words.

David knew that this meant trouble for him, and trouble seemed to be mounting up against him on every side.

Have you noticed that when you are discouraged, those around you seem to catch it? Discouragement is like a virus: if you stay around it, you may catch it.

That is why we need to watch what we hear, say and do. There are times when we may choose to help those in discouragement, but in doing so we must protect our hearts with God's Word, prayer and godly actions.

When I was struggling to deal with the death of three family members, whenever discouragement tried to attach itself to me, the one thing I remained constant in was prayer. Even when I slacked off in my Bible reading and fellowshipping with others, I prayed — and God heard me and delivered me. He began to speak to me and give me instruction. He brought the Word up within me to revive me and heal me from the inside outward.

Communication with God is vital when in discouragement.

David knew this truth, and when he prayed, God began to move — not all at once, but He did begin to move.

## God Sends David a Friend and Ally

**And it came to pass, that when David was come to the top of the mount, where he worshipped God, behold, Hushai the Archite came to meet him with his coat rent, and earth upon his head:**

**Unto whom David said, If thou passest on with me, then thou shalt be a burden unto me:**

**But if thou return to the city, and say unto Absalom, I will be thy servant, O king; as I have been thy father's servant hitherto, so will I now also be thy servant: then mayest thou for me defeat the counsel of Ahithophel.**

**And hast thou not there with thee Zadok and Abiathar the priests? therefore it shall be, that what**

thing soever thou shalt hear out of the king's house, thou shalt tell it to Zadok and Abiathar the priests.

Behold, they have there with them their two sons, Ahimaaz Zadok's son, and Jonathan Abiathar's son; and by them ye shall send unto me every thing that ye can hear.

So Hushai David's friend came into the city, and Absalom came into Jerusalem.

2 Samuel 15:32-37

God began with encouragement and then proceeded to walk David through to victory.

He will do the same for you.

## God Provides

And when David was a little past the top of the hill, behold, Ziba the servant of Mephibosheth met him, with a couple of asses saddled, and upon them two hundred loaves of bread, and an hundred bunches of raisins, and an hundred of summer fruits, and a bottle of wine.

And the king said unto Ziba, What meanest thou by these? And Ziba said, The asses be for the king's household to ride on; and the bread and summer fruit for the young men to eat; and the wine, that such as be faint in the wilderness may drink.

2 Samuel 16:1,2

God moved in David's life through Ziba, the servant of Mephibosheth who was the son of Jonathan, David's best friend. (2 Sam. 4:4.) David had shown kindness to Mephibosheth (2 Sam. 9:1-13.) Now his servant Ziba came to David with provisions — donkeys to ride, bread and fruit to eat and wine to drink. This provision brought rest for those who were weary, food for those who hungered and drink for those who were faint.

As we pray in the hard times, God provides for us.

Always look for God's provision in the wilderness as you pray. He has a way for you to survive those trying times. He can bring the most unlikely people to provide what you need, just as He used the servant Ziba.

You might think that when provision comes, your troubles are over, but that is not necessarily so. It just means that God is moving in your behalf to bring you through to victory, so don't give up. Also remember that your enemy doesn't play fair, so don't assume he will. When you are down is when he loves to attack.

Remember that God is with you, and for you, even when you are down. He will pick you up and direct your footsteps if you will allow Him to lead you. If you don't, you will become weary and depressed.

## Refresh Yourself!

And when king David came to Bahurim, behold, thence came out a man of the family of the house of Saul, whose name was Shimei, the son of Gera: he came forth, and cursed still as he came.

And cast stones at David, and at all the servants of king David: and all the people and all the mighty men were on his right hand and on his left.

And thus said Shimei when he cursed, Come out, come out, thou bloody man, and thou man of Belial:

The Lord hath returned upon thee all the blood of the house of Saul, in whose stead thou hast reigned; and the Lord hath delivered the kingdom into the hand of Absalom thy son: and, behold, thou art taken in thy mischief, because thou art a bloody man.

Then said Abishai the son of Zeruiah unto the king, Why should this dead dog curse my lord the king? let me go over, I pray thee, and take off his head.

And the king said, What have I to do with you, ye sons of Zeruiah? so let him curse, because the Lord hath said unto him, Curse David. Who shall then say, Wherefore hast thou done so?

And David said to Abishai, and to all his servants, Behold, my son, which came forth of my bowels, seeketh my life: how much more now may this Benjamite do it? let him alone, and let him curse; for the Lord hath bidden him.

It may be that the Lord will look on mine affliction, and that the Lord will requite me good for his cursing this day.

And as David and his men went by the way, Shimei went along on the hill's side over against him, and cursed as he went, and threw stones at him, and cast dust.

And the king, and all the people that were with him, came weary, and refreshed themselves there.
**2 Samuel 16:5-14**

Shimei, one of Saul's family members, began to curse David, throw stones at him and call him names. This kind of abuse is hard to take when you are already discouraged. David began to allow it to affect him. He let this man continue to follow him, cursing him and saying bad things about him, tossing rocks and throwing dirt on him, so he arrived at his destination very weary.

But in verse 14 we read that David refreshed himself there. King David refreshed himself in his weariness.

Just because you are down and weary for a time doesn't mean you have to stay that way.

Refresh yourself!

## A Glad Heart Is Better Than Good Things

**Thou hast put gladness in my heart, more than in the time that their corn and their wine increased.**
**Psalm 4:7**

Now remember where David was and what was going on, yet he still said, "A glad heart means more than all the good things of the land."

I can tell you from experience that you can have the good things of this land. But if you do not have a glad heart, you will not really enjoy them or even care that you have them.

You cannot buy what God will freely give, as you refresh yourself in Him.

## God Gives Rest and Peace

**I will both lay me down in peace, and sleep: for thou, Lord, only makest me dwell in safety.**
**Psalm 4:8**

David was weary and yet he declared, "God will give me rest and peace." He had been running, his enemy was trying to kill him and people were cursing him. He was overwhelmed, yet he still believed that God would give him rest. He knew the rest would come as he refreshed himself in the Lord.

This rest and refreshing cannot come through someone else, but must come straight from God, by spending time with Him. It pays to go to God when it seems there is no way. Not only will He give you rest and peace, but He will keep you from harm and show you the way.

How wonderful when God Himself replaces sadness with gladness in our hearts — right in the midst of discouragement, depression, despondency and despair.

## A Good Word Makes a Glad Heart

**Heaviness in the heart of man maketh it stoop: but a good word maketh it glad.**
**Proverbs 12:25**

Here the writer of Proverbs talks about the heart of man, saying that it is a good word which makes it glad.

In the Bible we have a good word if we will but look at it and wait for it in the wilderness of discouragement.

Be refreshed in the Lord and receive a glad heart from His Word.

## Arrived Weary, Left Refreshed

David may have arrived weary, but through communion with God he soon began to see victory. By faith he didn't stay weary, and you don't have to either.

In Isaiah 40:29 the prophet wrote of the Lord, "He giveth power to the faint; and to them that have no might he increaseth strength."

God wants you to win and to experience victory. If there is a problem, you can take care of your part by going to the Lord. As Peter told the people of his day: "Repent ye therefore, and be converted, that your sins may be blotted out, when the times of refreshing shall come from the presence of the Lord."

God has refreshing for you in His presence. (Ps. 16:11.)

Go get it!

## The Counsel of Ahithophel

And the counsel of Ahithophel, which he counselled in those days, was as if a man had inquired at the oracle of God; so was all the counsel of Ahithophel both with David and with Absalom.

Moreover Ahithophel said unto Absalom, Let me now choose out twelve thousand men, and I will arise and pursue after David this night:

And I will come upon him while he is weary and weak handed, and will make him afraid: and all the people that are with him shall flee; and I will smite the king only:

And I will bring back all the people unto thee: the man whom thou seekest is as if all returned: so all the people shall be in peace.

And the saying pleased Absalom well, and all the elders of Israel.

**2 Samuel 16:23; 17:1-4**

So Absalom began to wage war against his father David to destroy him. After driving David and his followers out of Jerusalem and setting himself on the throne of Israel, Absalom called upon his father's former counselor Ahithophel for advice on what to do next.

In times past, the counsel of Ahithophel had been "as if a man had inquired at the oracle of God." But now that he had betrayed King David and had joined Absalom's rebellion, he had made himself the enemy of God — which sealed his doom.

## Hushai's Counsel

> Then said Absalom, Call now Husahi the Archite also, and let us hear likewise what he saith.
>
> And when Husahi was come to Absalom, Absalom spake unto him, saying, Ahithophel hath spoken after this manner: shall we do after his saying? if not; speak thou.
>
> And Husahi said unto Absalom, The counsel that Ahithophel hath given is not good at this time....
>
> Therefore I counsel that all Israel be generally gathered unto thee, from Dan even to Beersheba, as the sand that is by the sea for multitude; and that thou go to battle in thine own person....
>
> And Absalom and all the men of Israel said, The counsel of Hushai the Archite is better than the counsel of Ahithophel. For the Lord had appointed to defeat the good counsel of Ahithophel, to the intent that the Lord might bring evil upon Absalom.
>
> **2 Samuel 17:5-7,11,14**

After hearing the advice of Ahithophel, Absalom called in Hushai, David's friend. Hushai had returned to the palace in Jerusalem to spy on Absalom and report to David what Absalom was planning.

Of course, when Husahi was asked by Absalom what to do, he spoke against the counsel given by Ahithophel. He told Absalom that instead of allowing Ahithophel to take twelve thousand men and hunt down David, Absalom should organize a huge army of Israelites and lead it himself.

That advice pleased Absalom and his men, so they rejected the counsel given by Ahithophel, just as David had prayed. (2 Sam. 15:31). The Lord made Ahithophel's words foolishness to Absalom, in keeping with Ahithophel's name, which means in Hebrew "brother of folly."[1]

Neither Absalom nor Ahithophel knew that Hushai, at the direction of the Lord, was setting both of them up for defeat and destruction.

## The End of Ahithophel

Then said Hushai unto Zadok and to Abiathar the priests, Thus and thus did Ahithophel counsel Absalom and the elders of Israel; and thus and thus have I counselled.

Now therefore send quickly, and tell David, saying, Lodge not this night in the plains of the wilderness, but speedily pass over; lest the king be swallowed up, and all the people that are with him....

Then David arose, and all the people that were with him, and they passed over Jordan: by the morning light there lacked not one of them that was not gone over Jordan.

And when Ahithophel saw that his counsel was not followed, he saddled his ass, and arose, and gat him home to his house, to his city, and put his household in order, and hanged himself, and died, and was buried in the sepulchre of his father.

Then David came to Mahanaim. And Absalom passed over Jordan, he and all the men of Israel with him.

**2 Samuel 17:15,16,22-24**

---

[1]James Strong, *Strong's Exhaustive Concordance of the Bible* (Nashville: Abingdon, 1890), "Hebrew and Chaldee Dictionary," p. 11, entry #302.

Hushai sent word to David of what had happened in the palace, how Absalom had listened to his counsel rather than that of Ahithophel. He warned David to take his people and flee, because Absalom and his army would be coming after them to destroy them — which was all part of the trap that the Lord was laying for the enemies of David.

When Ahithophel, who had always been the respected counselor to the king of Israel, saw that his counsel was no longer being followed, he realized that he had ruined himself by going over to David's enemy. Filled with remorse and regret, like Judas, he could not live with his betrayal of his master and so, also like Judas, he went out and hanged himself.

## God's Continued Provision

**And it came to pass, when David was come to Mahanaim, that Shobi the son of Nahash of Rabbah, of the children of Ammon, and Machir the son of Ammiel of Lo-debar, and Barzillai the Gileadite of Rogelim,**

**Brought beds, and basons, and earthen vessels, and wheat, and barley, and flour, and parched corn, and beans, and lentiles, and parched pulse,**

**And honey, and butter, and sheep, and cheese of kine, for David, and for the people that were with him, to eat: for they said, The people is hungry, and weary, and thirsty, in the wilderness.**

**2 Samuel 17:27-29**

After fleeing from Absalom for a second time, David and his people were again hungry, weary and thirsty. And so once again God made provision for them.

No matter how difficult your situation may be, God will make provision for you in the wilderness of discouragement. You may be in the wilderness, just as David was, but like David, you are about to come out. To do that, God wants you strong, just as He wanted David and his men strong to face the coming battle.

## God's Provision of People

> And David numbered the people that were with him, and set captains of thousands, and captains of hundreds over them.
>
> And David sent forth a third part of the people under the hand of Joab, and a third part under the hand of Abishai the son of Zeruiah, Joab's brother, and a third part under the hand of Ittai the Gittite. And the king said unto the people, I will surely go forth with you myself also.
>
> But the people answered, Thou shalt not go forth: for if we flee away, they will not care for us; neither if half of us die, will they care for us: but now thou art worth ten thousand of us: therefore now it is better that thou succour us out of the city.
>
> And the king said unto them, What seemeth you best I will do. And the king stood by the gate side, and all the people came out by hundreds and by thousands.
>
> And the king commanded Joab and Abishai and Ittai, saying, Deal gently for my sake with the young man, even with Absalom. And all the people heard when the king gave all the captains charge concerning Absalom.
>
> **2 Samuel 18:1-5**

Not only will God provide for your hunger, weariness, and thirst, He will also provide the people you need to help you fight your way out of that time of discouragement.

In verse 2 of this passage we read about Ittai, the Gittite, one of David's commanders. This was the man who had attached himself to David during his hard time, as we are told in 2 Samuel 15:18-22:

> And all his servants passed on beside him; and all the Cherethites, and all the Pelethites, and all the Gittites, six hundred men which came after him from Gath, passed on before the king.

> Then said the king to Ittai the Gittite, Wherefore goest thou also with us? return to thy place, and abide with the king: for thou art a stranger, and also an exile.
>
> Whereas thou camest but yesterday, should I this day make thee go up and down with us? seeing I go whither I may, return thou, and take back thy brethren: mercy and truth be with thee.
>
> And Ittai answered the king, and said, As the Lord liveth, and as my lord the king liveth, surely in what place my lord the king shall be, whether in death or life, even there also will thy servant be.
>
> And David said to Ittai, Go and pass over. And Ittai the Gittite passed over, and all his men, and all the little ones that were with him.

This man Ittai was a Gittite, meaning that he was from Gath. Like many others in David's company, he was a "stranger," that is, a foreigner (actually a Philistine).[2]

He had only been with David for a short time, but something about David must have bound Ittai to him, for he swore his loyalty to the king and proved himself loyal.

## God's Refreshment

**For we have great joy and consolation in thy love, because the bowels of the saints are refreshed by thee....**
**Philemon 7**

God has people like Ittai for you. They may not understand why, but they find themselves attached to you and want to help you.

I call such associations "divine connections." In other words, they are connections established by God for further or later assistance.

I have experienced such "divine connections" many times in my life, and I find that they continue through the years.

---

[2] *The New Oxford Annotated Bible* (New York: Oxford University Press, 1962, 1973), p. 395, footnotes to 2 Samuel 15:13-18.

Why?

Because they are ordained of God.

If you do not recognize these "divine connections," you may reject them because of their outward appearance, their lack of influence or their different personality traits. As a result, when such people should be helping you, they are not there; likewise, when they have need of you, you are not around.

Follow God's leading. As with David, He has people to help you, and people you need to help, as you both fulfill His calling.

God will provide what you need to win your battle over discouragement. Just refresh yourself in Him. When I speak of refreshing yourself I mean praying, communing, fellowshipping with the Lord and reading the Word. This kind of activity will keep you in His presence, which is where true refreshment is found.

## The End of Absalom and the Rebellion

>So the people went out into the field against Israel: and the battle was in the wood of Ephraim;
>
>Where the people of Israel were slain before the servants of David, and there was there a great slaughter that day of twenty thousand men.
>
>For the battle was there scattered over the face of all the country: and the wood devoured more people that day than the sword devoured.
>
>And Absalom met the servants of David. And Absalom rode upon a mule, and the mule went under the thick boughs of a great oak, and his head caught hold of the oak, and he was taken up between the heaven and the earth; and the mule that was under him went away.
>
>And a certain man saw it, and told Joab, and said, Behold, I saw Absalom hanged in an oak....

> Then said Joab, I may not tarry thus with thee. And he took three darts in his hand, and thrust them through the heart of Absalom, while he was yet alive in the midst of the oak.
>
> And ten young men that bare Joab's armour compassed about and smote Absalom, and slew him.
>
> And Joab blew the trumpet, and the people returned from pursuing after Israel: for Joab held back the people.
>
> And they took Absalom, and cast him into a great pit in the wood, and laid a very great heap of stones upon him: and Israel fled every one to his tent.
>
> 2 Samuel 18:6-10,14-17

During the battle against the forces of his father, King David, Absalom was left hanging, along with his rebellion. His support (his mule) left him all alone, suspended between heaven and earth.

That is the fate of those in rebellion. They will be left hanging between heaven and earth with no one to turn to for help.

## David Returns and Is Restored

> So the king returned, and came to Jordan. And Judah came to Gilgal, to go to meet the king, to conduct the king over Jordan.
>
> 2 Samuel 19:15

Once Absalom was destroyed, his rebellion fell apart. All those who had followed him came back to David who returned to Jerusalem where he was restored to his throne.

I believe this situation turned around because David *prayed* and *stayed* in God's presence when discouragement came. He *chose* to turn to God instead of turning to discouragement. He *rehearsed* Who God was and what He would do. He *believed*, regardless of his circumstances, and it was then that his restoration began.

Does this mean that David never had to deal with trouble or discouragement again? No, but by staying in God, Who never changes, David stayed refreshed instead of discouraged.

You can stay refreshed and not discouraged by making a choice. Choose to *refresh yourself* in God's presence. Rehearse Who God is and what He has done for you. Believe His report — His Word — regardless of circumstances.

God wants to bring restoration to you, just as He did to David.

David went through a very hard and discouraging time in his life and lived to see the goodness of the Lord.

That same goodness is available to you.

## Run the Race With Endurance

In closing, I would like to leave you a few Scripture passages to lean on and be encouraged by. The first is Psalm 42:5,6 NAS:

**Why are you in despair, O my soul?**
**And why have you become disturbed within me?**
**Hope in God, for I shall again praise Him**
**For the help of His presence.**
**O my God, my soul is in despair within me;**
**Therefore I remember Thee from the land of the Jordan,**
**And the peaks of Hermon, from Mount Mizar.**

Like the psalmist, when we are faced with discouraging, disheartening situations, we need to remind ourselves Whom we serve and all He has done for us in the past.

Whenever discouragement tries to come and overwhelm you, put yourself in remembrance of the God you serve and of the blessings that are yours in Him.

In Psalm 61:1,2 NAS we read these words from King David:

> Hear my cry, O God;
> Give heed to my prayer.
> From the end of the earth I call to Thee,
> when my heart is faint;
> Lead me to the rock that is higher than I.

We have talked about rocks as troubles. Now we need to consider the Rock, which is Jesus Christ, that is higher than we, the Rock that is higher than any trouble in this world.

Remember, if that Rock is higher than you, it is higher than any obstacle that may block your path, higher than any problem that may come against you.

Finally, in Hebrews 12:1,2 NAS we are told:

> Therefore, since we have so great a cloud of witnesses surrounding us, let us also lay aside every encumbrance, and the sin which so easily entangles us, and let us run with endurance the race that is set before us,
>
> fixing our eyes on Jesus, the author and perfecter of faith, who for the joy set before Him endured the cross, despising the shame, and has sat down at the right hand of the throne of God.

We are to run with endurance the race that is set before us. How do we do that? By fixing our eyes on Jesus, Whom the *King James Version* calls "the author and finisher of our faith." (See Heb. 12:2.)

If you are going to walk out of discouragement, you are going to have to fix your eyes on the Lord and run with endurance the race that He has set before you.

I know that discouragement has touched many in the body of Christ, but I want you to know that for every type of discouragement, God has an answer. No matter what has happened to discourage you in your life, God has a solution for you, just as He did for the Old Testament characters whose lives we have studied in this book.

## A Final Word

When Elijah was alone, separated and running for his life, he had to stand on the mountain before God. He had to go to the Lord and seek for the answer to his discouraging situation.

God told him, "Turn around, go back and finish what you started. Don't be afraid. I will go with you to help you and empower you."

Once Elijah was obedient to the Lord, once he took the steps God had told him to take, he found himself walking back in victory, fulfilling the call of God on his life.

When Moses became worn out and discouraged because of the heavy burden of responsibility for the people of God, like Elijah he wanted to die. But also like Elijah, once he turned to the Lord and prepared himself to hear what the Lord had to say to him, God gave him a very simple solution to what had been causing him so much trouble — "Delegate authority."

When Reuben and Gad began to discourage the rest of the Children of Israel by trying to settle for the suitable, once again God gave Moses a simple solution to the problem: "Have them fight with their brothers to take Canaan, then they can come back and take up their possessions on the far side of the Jordan." (Num. 32:20-32.)

When the Hebrew spies came back from scouting out the Promised Land and gave an "evil report" about it, discouraging the people from going in and taking possession of their rightful inheritance, once again the solution was simple. Caleb and Joshua were to keep their eyes fixed and focused on God to take them through to the fulfillment of the promise as they followed the Lord fully.

When the Children of Israel were denied passage across his land by the king of Edom and became discouraged because of the irritations, discomforts and troubles along the way, they complained to the Lord Who sent a plague among them. After they had repented and returned to the Lord, He gave them victories over other kings who had also opposed their passage. (Num. 20-21.)

When David faced discouragement because of the rebellion of his own son and the betrayal, ridicule and opposition of many in his kingdom, he overcame it by refreshing himself in the Lord, trusting Him to fulfill His plan and purpose for him.

Like the doubters and complainers among the Children of Israel, many people may try to talk you out of the promises of God, which will cause you to become discouraged. But allow God to be God. He is the One Who will carry you through to the fulfillment of His promises.

In Romans 3:3,4 NAS the Apostle Paul wrote of such people, "What then? If some did not believe, their unbelief will not nullify the faithfulness of God, will it? May it never be! Rather, let God be found true, though every man be found a liar, as it is written."

When you find yourself with people who are saying things to get you to settle for the suitable, when you find yourself being discouraged by the sayings of others, when you find yourself being opposed and oppressed by your enemies, remember the sayings of God. It is being filled with and yielded to the Word and Spirit of God that will carry you through to victory.

In times of discouragement, wrap yourself in the Word of God rather than the words of men. Develop a close relationship and fellowship with Him. We must have relationship and fellowship with other people, but our relationship and fellowship with God must come first and foremost.

When you run into detours on the journey, when you encounter sand, gravel and rocks along the way, don't become discouraged and give up. Instead, just make sure you are being continually filled with spiritual food and water and are wielding your spiritual authority.

Keep your eyes on the goal, not the ground.

I remember when our children were small. When we would set out on a trip, as long as their little tummies were full and there was water in the car to drink, they were happy. But as soon as they got hungry or thirsty, they would begin to mumble and grumble. When they began to whine and complain, it magnified the sand, the gravel and the rocks in the road.

Remember, your attitude determines how you handle discouraging situations. A bad attitude can be truly and permanently altered through God, by feeding on His Word and by drinking of His Spirit.

Keep yourself in the love of God and in the Word and prayer. When you are tempted to walk away from God, that is the very time you need to look more directly in His face through those means.

I can guarantee you that the enemy is going to try to discourage you in your walk of faith, just as he tried to do with Elijah, with Moses, with the Children of Israel and with David in their walks. It was only when they acknowledged God and listened to Him that they were able to resist the devil and move on to victory.

I don't mean to imply that discouragement is not real or that because you are a believer you will never have to deal with it. Discouragement *is* real, and each of us will have to deal with it all of our lives.

In my own ministry, I have been attacked by discouragement. The enemy has often sent discouraging people and circumstances to try to neutralize me, to stop me, to defeat me, just as he has with you. But I chose not to be *discouraged* and to be *encouraged* by believing the Word of God and by dwelling in His presence!

I am telling you that if you turn to God and away from discouragement, the Lord has the solution — no matter what the situation.

If discouraging people are saying negative things to you or about you, turn to God and listen to what He has to say. Get your thoughts, your emotions, your words and your actions in line with His Word, not the saying of men.

I realize that the solutions for the problem of discouragement that I have given you in this book may seem very simple, but they do work. I encourage you not to take them as an oversimplification, but as a *lifeline*, for only a touch of the Spirit can give life. Hold on. You just need a touch of God's power, and you find it *in* Him.

Stay in the Word and in prayer, yielding yourself to what God is saying to you. Embrace what He is saying, yield to it, lean on it, allow it to change you. No matter what direction you receive, follow it *fully*. Through the Word take authority over the enemy, instead of allowing the enemy to have authority over you. Take that first step of faith, and God will walk you step by step out of discouragement and defeat into joy and victory.

# Conclusion: Comfort and Counsel of the Holy Spirit

> **Wherefore, my beloved, as ye have always obeyed, not as in my presence only, but now much more in my absence, work out your own salvation with fear and trembling.**
>
> **For it is God which worketh in you both to will and to do of his good pleasure.**
>
> Philippians 2:12,13

When you experience times of discouragement, whether brought on by the sayings of others, the burden of responsibility, settling for the suitable, troubles along the way, rebellion against you or some other situation, you need someone to talk to. You will soon discover, however, that not everyone wants to listen to you.

One of the ways to get through discouragement caused by grief is to talk about the one being grieved. Unfortunately, it seems that other people, even our closest friends and family members, are able to give us only so much of their time and concern; after that, they tend to lose interest. It is as if a deadline for recovery is drawn; a certain time limit is set for us to "get over it and get on with life."

The problem is that our emotions do not work on a schedule or by a timetable. Recovery from discouragement and depression is often a long process, and if we depend only on other people for comfort and counsel, many times we will not receive all the help we need.

When you are going through an extended period of discouragement, depression or despondency you need to turn to the Holy Spirit within you. He is patient and will help you as long as you need Him. People may grow tired of hearing over and over again the same story concerning your loved one, but God will never tire of giving you His mercy, love and grace when you are hurting.

Although your discouragement or depression may not stem from grief, the Holy Spirit is the same Comforter for all of life's problems that bring a sense of helplessness and hopelessness. He is always ready to help you, not only during trying times, such as grief over the loss of a loved one, but in the normal events of everyday life.

When you are experiencing discouragement, you will be tempted to neglect reading your Bible, to quit praying and to stop paying attention to spiritual things. But you must not do so! If you do, you will fill your hours with worldly things and will begin to look only to other people to help you overcome your depressed condition.

At such times, do not turn from trusting God, but turn to Him; He is always ready to help you.

Although people are often kind and sympathetic, and many good counseling materials are available and helpful, do not limit yourself to these aids. Go to God first, open up the lines of communication with Him, and then keep them open through prayer, Bible reading and meditation. Allow the Holy Spirit to minister to you, and draw on His tremendous power to work in you and to bring you through discouragement to victory.

## About the Author

**Nancy Gray** is an ordained minister and president of Nancy Gray Ministries. With the assistance and support of her husband Don, she is able to fulfill the call of God upon her life. Nancy ministers throughout the United States in churches, seminars, conventions and women's organizations. Ministry in Canada and overseas has allowed her tapes and books to bless many people throughout the world.

Nancy is a precious woman of God who teaches the Word in a clear and understandable manner, moving in the gifts of the Spirit with sensitivity. She ministers to the whole body, as she has a heart for the local church and understands the importance of a sound relationship between pastor and congregation. With this understanding, she is able to minister and ignite to excitement the body of Christ wherever she goes. Many who hear her teach begin to experience victory and to live for Jesus as never before.

For further information or assistance, contact Nancy at:

Nancy Gray Ministries
P.O. Box 470171
Tulsa, Oklahoma 74147

*Please include your prayer requests
and comments when you write.*

For additional copies of this book contact:

**Harrison House**
P. O. Box 35035
Tulsa, Oklahoma 74153

In Canada contact:

Word Alive
P. O. Box 670
Niverville, Manitoba
CANADA R0A 1E0

## The Harrison House Vision

Proclaiming the truth and the power
Of the Gospel of Jesus Christ
With excellence;

Challenging Christians to
Live victoriously,
Grow spiritually,
Know God intimately.